Better Homes and Gardens®

QUILT-LOVERS' FAVORITES®

FROM AMERICAN PATCHWORK & QUILTING™

Better Homes and Gardens® Creative Collection®
Des Moines, Iowa

VOLUME 9

Editorial Director	JOHN RIHA
Editor in Chief	DEBORAH GORE OHRN
Art Director	BRENDA DRAKE LESCH
Group Editor	JENNIFER ERBE KELTNER
Managing Editor	KATHLEEN ARMENTROUT

Better Homes and Gardens®

QUILT-LOVERS' FAVORITES

FROM AMERICAN PATCHWORK & QUILTING.

Editors ELIZABETH TISINGER AND JILL ABELOE MEAD		*Design Director* NANCY WILES	
Assistant Editor JODY SANDERS		*Senior Graphic Designer* ELIZABETH STUMBO	
Interactive Editor	LISA SCHUMACHER		
Administrative Assistant	MARY IRISH		

Contributing Quilt Tester	LAURA BOEHNKE
Contributing Technical Editor	LILA SCOTT
Contributing Project Designer	JAN RAGALLER
Contributing Graphic Designer	JANN WILLIAMS
Contributing Copy Editors	MARIA DURYEE AND MARY HELEN SCHILTZ
Contributing Proofreader	ANGELA INGLE
Contributing Writers	DIANE DORO AND ANGELA INGLE
Contributing Technical Illustrators	DRAFAHL DESIGN CO. AND CHRIS NEUBAUER GRAPHICS
Contributing Photo Stylists	TARI COLBY AND JANN WILLIAMS
Contributing Watercolor Illustrator	ANN WEISS
Group Director, Premedia/Quality Operations	STEVE JOHNSON
Senior Director, Premedia Services	PENNY SULLIVAN
Color Quality Analyst	PAM POWERS
Prepress Desktop Specialist	PATRICIA J. SAVAGE
Photo Studio Manager	JEFF ANDERSON
Consumer Products Marketing Director	STEVE SWANSON
Consumer Products Marketing Manager	WENDY MERICAL
Business Manager	JAMES LEONARD
Production Director	DOUGLAS M. JOHNSTON

Executive Vice President	DOUG OLSON
Vice President and General Manager, SIP	JEFF MYERS
Vice President, Retail Sales	DAVID ALGIRE
Brand Manager	MARK MOOBERRY
Marketing Director, Meredith Direct	HEATHER PROCTOR

Meredith Publishing Group

President	JACK GRIFFIN
Chief Revenue Officer	TOM HARTY
Finance and Administration	MIKE RIGGS
Manufacturing	BRUCE HESTON
Consumer Marketing	DAVE BALL
Corporate Sales	MICHAEL BROWNSTEIN
Meredith 360°	JEANNINE SHAO COLLINS
Interactive Media	DOUG OLSON
Interactive Media Sales	LAUREN WIENER
Corporate Marketing	NANCY WEBER
Research	BRITTA WARE
Chief Technology Officer	TINA STEIL
New Media Marketing Services	ANDY WILSON

ℳeredith CORPORATION

President and Chief Executive Officer   STEPHEN M. LACY

Chairman of the Board   WILLIAM T. KERR

In Memoriam – E.T. MEREDITH III, 1933–2003

CHOOSING FAVORITES

*Favorite. As a noun, the word signifies preference, choice, or star.
As an adjective, it means chosen, favored, or especially liked.
To us, the word describes the projects that fill our latest edition,
Volume 9, of* Quilt-Lovers' Favorites®.

*In the pages that follow, we take another look at 15 of our readers'
favorite patterns from past issues of* American Patchwork &
Quilting® *magazine and sister publications. To sweeten the deal,
we add 29 all-new projects using the blocks, units, borders, or
appliqué shapes from the original quilts. You'll find projects of
all sizes—from pillows to messenger bags, table toppers to wall
hangings, and comfy throws to bed-size quilts.*

*As always, full-size patterns, numerous color options, and our
reference guide to quiltmaking, Quilter's Schoolhouse, are included
to aid you in making these projects. Optional size charts are
provided for many projects, making the math easy and helping
you modify the designs to suit your needs.*

*My guess is that you'll find it difficult to choose which of these
quilts is your favorite. I did, so I'll be making several of the
projects for family and friends. Most of all, I hope you enjoy
time spent on your favorite hobby—quilting!*

Jennifer

Jennifer Erbe Keltner
Group Editor, American Patchwork & Quilting

3

TABLE *of* CONTENTS

5

20

8

34

30

TIMELESS CLASSICS

Passing traditions from generation to generation is one enjoyable aspect of quilting. The art of quiltmaking and the classic patterns themselves often evoke fond memories for quilters. Using today's techniques, re-create the ageless beauties on the following pages to make quilts your family and friends will treasure for years to come.

IRISH
Cabins

Using strip sets speeds the piecing when replicating an antique quilt

from the collection of quilt shop owner Julie Hendricksen.

Materials

3 yards muslin (blocks, sashing, pieced border)

4—18×22" pieces (fat quarters) assorted light prints, stripes, and shirtings (blocks, sashing, pieced border)

14—18×22" pieces (fat quarters) assorted tan prints and dark prints, stripes, and shirtings in blue, red, and black (blocks, sashing, pieced border)

1⅞ yards pink stripe (blocks, sashing, pieced border)

2⅛ yards black-and-white shirting (sashing, borders, binding)

5 yards backing fabric

83×89" batting

Finished quilt: 77×83"
Finished block: 19½×22½"
For additional quilt sizes, see Optional Sizes chart on Pattern Sheet 2.

Quantities are for 44/45"-wide, 100% cotton fabrics. Measurements include ¼" seam allowances. Sew with right sides together unless otherwise stated.

Historical Notes

To re-create the look of the original quilt, in which some of the dark prints have faded to tan, the following instructions specify mixing up dark and tan prints in the same positions in the block.

For a scrappier look, consider piecing segments with individual squares and rectangles. See **Block Assembly Diagram**, *page 12,* for placement ideas.

Cut Fabrics

Cut pieces in the following order. Before cutting pink stripe, note stripe orientation in diagrams 3, 5, 7, 9, and 12; cut strips so stripes run in correct direction in each strip set.

From muslin, cut:
- 1—17×21" strip
- 4—8×21" strips
- 60—2×21" strips

From assorted light prints, stripes, and shirtings, cut:
- 26—2×21" strips

From remaining muslin and assorted light prints, stripes, and shirtings, cut:
- 52—2" squares

From assorted tan prints and dark prints, stripes, and shirtings, cut:
- 103—2×21" strips
- 48—2" squares

From pink stripe, cut:
- 1—17×21" strip
- 4—11×21" strips
- 4—5×21" strips

From black-and-white shirting, cut:
- 9—2½×42" binding strips
- 5—2×42" strips for border
- 4—14×21" strips

continued

Assemble Block Segments

Strip Set 1

Referring to **Diagram 1**, sew together three muslin or light print 2×21" strips and four tan or dark print 2×21" strips to make strip set 1. Press seams toward tan or dark print strips. Repeat to make six total of strip set 1. Cut strip sets into 54—2"-wide segments total.

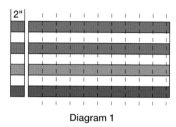

Diagram 1

Strip Set 2

Referring to **Diagram 2**, sew together four muslin or light print 2×21" strips and three tan or dark print 2×21" strips to make strip set 2. Press seams toward tan or dark print strips. Repeat to make five total of strip set 2. Cut strip sets into 45—2"-wide segments total.

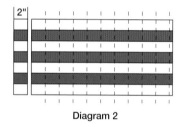

Diagram 2

Strip Set 3

Referring to **Diagram 3**, sew together two muslin or light print 2×21" strips, two tan or dark print 2×21" strips, and one pink stripe 5×21" strip to make strip set 3. Press seams toward tan or dark print strips. Repeat to make a second strip set 3. Cut strip sets into 18—2"-wide segments total.

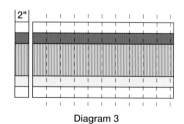

Diagram 3

Strip Set 4

Referring to **Diagram 4**, sew together one muslin 8×21" strip and two tan or dark print 2×21" strips to make strip set 4. Press seams toward tan or dark print strips. Repeat to make a second strip set 4. Cut strip sets into 18—2"-wide segments total.

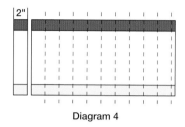

Diagram 4

Strip Set 5

Referring to **Diagram 5**, join six muslin or light print 2×21" strips, six tan or dark print 2×21" strips, and one pink stripe 5×21" strip to make strip set 5. Press seams toward tan or dark prints. Repeat to make a second strip set 5. Cut strip sets into 18—2"-wide segments total.

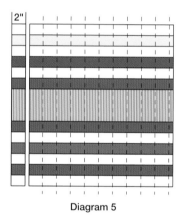

Diagram 5

Strip Set 6

Referring to **Diagram 6**, join one muslin 8×21" strip, four muslin or light print 2×21" strips, and six tan or dark print 2×21" strips to make strip set 6. Press seams toward tan or dark print strips. Repeat to make a second strip set 6. Cut strip sets into 18—2"-wide segments total.

Strip Set 7

Referring to **Diagram 7**, sew together four muslin or light print 2×21" strips, four tan or dark print 2×21" strips, and one pink stripe 11×21" strip to make strip set 7. Press seams toward tan or dark print strips. Repeat to make a second strip set 7. Cut strip sets into 18—2"-wide segments total.

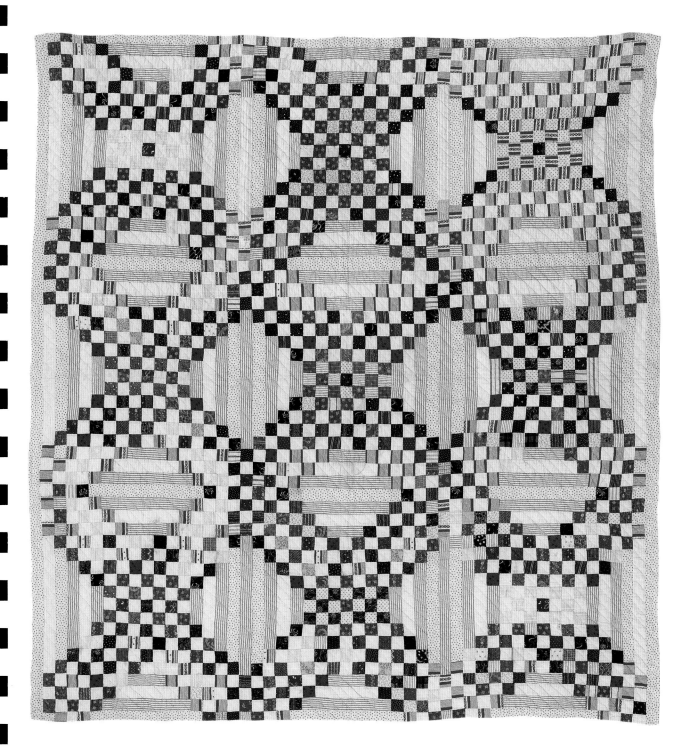

2"

Diagram 6

2"

Diagram 7

continued

Assemble Blocks

1. Referring to **Block Assembly Diagram**, lay out six strip set 1 segments, five strip set 2 segments, and two segments *each* from strip sets 3 through 7 in three sections.

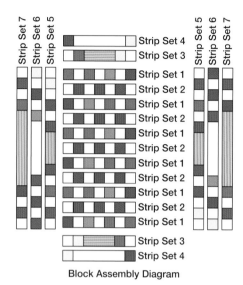

Block Assembly Diagram

2. Join segments in each section. Press seams in one direction. Join sections to make a block; press seams away from block center. The block should be 20×23" including seam allowances.

3. Repeat steps 1 and 2 to make nine blocks total.

Assemble Border and Sashing Segments

Strip Set 8

Referring to **Diagram 8**, sew together two muslin or light print 2×21" strips, two tan or dark print 2×21" strips, and one black-and-white shirting 14×21" strip to make strip set 8. Press seams toward black-and-white shirting. Repeat to make a second strip set 8. Cut strip sets into 12—2"-wide segments total.

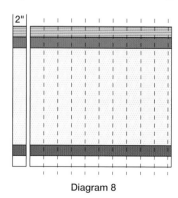

Diagram 8

Strip Set 9

Referring to **Diagram 9**, sew together two muslin or light print 2×21" strips, four tan or dark print 2×21" strips, and one pink stripe 11×21" strip to make strip set 9. Press seams toward tan or dark print strips. Repeat to make a second strip set 9. Cut strip sets into 18—2"-wide segments total.

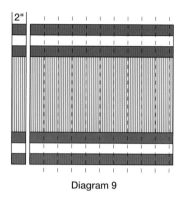

Diagram 9

Strip Set 10

Referring to **Diagram 10**, sew together two muslin or light print 2×21" strips, two tan or dark print 2×21" strips, and one muslin 17×21" strip to make strip set 10. Press seams toward tan or dark print strips. Cut strip set into six 2"-wide segments total.

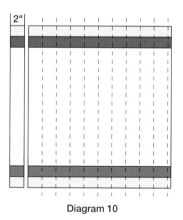

Diagram 10

Strip Set 11

Referring to **Diagram 11**, sew together two muslin or light print 2×21" strips, four tan or dark print 2×21" strips, and one black-and-white shirting 14×21" strip to make strip set 11. Press seams toward black-and-white shirting. Repeat to make a second strip set 11. Cut strip sets into 18—2"-wide segments total.

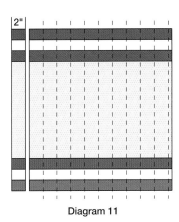

Diagram 11

Strip Set 12

Referring to **Diagram 12**, sew together two muslin or light print 2×21" strips, two tan or dark print 2×21" strips, and one pink stripe 17×21" strip to make strip set 12. Press seams away from pink stripe. Cut strip set into six 2"-wide segments total.

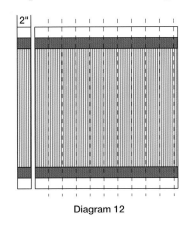

Diagram 12

Assemble Border and Sashing Units

1. Sew together one strip set 8 segment and one strip set 9 segment to make border unit A **(Diagram 13).** Press seam toward segment 8. Border unit A should be 3½×20" including seam allowances. Repeat to make six total of border unit A.

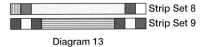

Diagram 13

2. Sew together one strip set 10 segment and one strip set 11 segment to make border unit B **(Diagram 14).** Press seam toward segment 10. Border unit B should be 3½×23" including seam allowances. Repeat to make six total of border unit B.

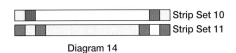

Diagram 14

3. Sew together two strip set 11 segments and one strip set 12 segment to make sashing unit C **(Diagram 15).** Press seams toward segment 12. Sashing unit C should be 5×23" including seam allowances. Repeat to make six total of sashing unit C.

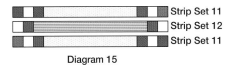

Diagram 15

4. Sew together two strip set 9 segments and one strip set 8 segment to make sashing unit D **(Diagram 16).** Press seams toward segment 8. Sashing unit D should be 5×20" including seam allowances. Repeat to make six total of sashing unit D.

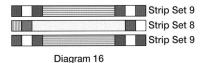

Diagram 16

5. Sew together two muslin or light print 2" squares and two assorted tan or dark print 2" squares in pairs **(Diagram 17).** Press seams toward tan or dark print squares. Join pairs to make a Four-Patch unit. Press seam in one direction. The Four-Patch unit should be 3½" square including seam allowances. Repeat to make four Four-Patch units total.

Diagram 17

6. Sew together three muslin or light print 2" squares and three tan or dark print 2" squares in two rows **(Diagram 18).** Press seams toward tan or dark print squares. Join rows to make a Six-Patch unit. Press seam in one direction. The Six-Patch unit should be 3½×5" including seam allowances. Repeat to make eight Six-Patch units total.

Diagram 18

continued

7. Sew together five muslin or light print 2" squares and four tan or dark print 2" squares in three rows **(Diagram 19)**. Press seams toward tan or dark print squares. Join rows to make a Nine-Patch unit. Press seams in one direction. The Nine-Patch unit should be 5" square including seam allowances. Repeat to make four Nine-Patch units total.

Diagram 19

Assemble Quilt Center

1. Referring to **Quilt Assembly Diagram**, lay out blocks, border units A and B, sashing units C and D, Four-Patch units, Six-Patch units, and Nine-Patch units in seven horizontal rows.

2. Sew together pieces in each row. Press seams in one direction, alternating direction with each row.

3. Join rows to make quilt center. Press seams in one direction. The quilt center should be 74×83" including seam allowances.

Add Border

1. Cut and piece black-and-white shirting 2×42" strips to make:
  • 2—2×83" border strips

2. Join border strips to long edges of quilt center to complete quilt top. Press seams toward border.

Finish Quilt

1. Layer quilt top, batting, and backing; baste. (For details, see Complete the Quilt, *page 159*.)

2. Quilt as desired. This antique quilt features hand-quilted diagonal lines at 1" intervals over the entire quilt top.

3. Bind with black-and-white shirting binding strips. (For details, see Complete the Quilt.)

Quilt Assembly Diagram

Irish Cabins

DOUBLE NINE-PATCH

Strip-piece the Nine-Patch blocks for a super-easy throw.

Materials

½ yard red print (blocks)

⅝ yard total assorted green and blue prints (blocks)

⅝ yard light green print (blocks)

⅞ yard cream-and-red floral (setting squares)

⅜ yard dark red print (inner border)

1 yard red tone-on-tone (outer border)

½ yard red-and-black print (binding)

3⅓ yards backing fabric

59" square batting

Finished quilt: 53" square
Finished block: 13½" square

Cut Fabrics

Cut pieces in the following order.

From red print, cut:
• 7—2×21" strips
• 4—2×11" strips

From assorted green and blue prints, cut:
• 14—2×21" strips
• 2—2×11" strips

From light green print, cut:
• 20—5" squares

From cream-and-red floral, cut:
• 4—14" squares

From dark red print, cut:
• 5—2×42" strips for inner border

From red tone-on-tone, cut:
• 5—5×42" strips for outer border

From red-and-black print, cut:
• 6—2½×42" binding strips

Assemble Blocks

1. Referring to **Diagram 20**, sew together one red print 2×21" strip and two assorted green or blue print 2×21" strips to make strip set 1. Press seams toward red print. Repeat to make three total of strip set 1. Cut strip sets into 25—2"-wide segments total.

Diagram 20
Strip Set 1

2. Referring to **Diagram 21**, sew together two red print 2×11" strips and one assorted green

Diagram 21
Strip Set 2

or blue print 2×11" strip to make strip set 2. Press seams toward red print strips. Repeat to make a second strip set 2. Cut strips sets into 10—2"-wide segments total.

3. Referring to **Diagram 22**, sew together one red print 2×21" strip and two assorted green or blue print 2×21" strips to make strip set 3. Press seams away from middle strip. Repeat to make four total of strip set 3. Cut strip sets into 40—2"-wide segments total.

Diagram 22
Strip Set 3

4. Sew together one strip set 1 segment and two strip set 3 segments to make unit A (**Diagram 23**). Press seams in one direction. Unit A should be 5" square including seam allowances. Repeat to make 20 total of unit A.

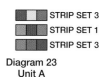

STRIP SET 3
STRIP SET 1
STRIP SET 3

Diagram 23
Unit A

5. Sew together one strip set 1 segment and two strip set 2 segments to make unit B (**Diagram 24**). Press seams in one direction. Unit B should be 5" square including seam allowances. Repeat to make five total of unit B.

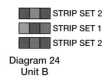

STRIP SET 2
STRIP SET 1
STRIP SET 2

Diagram 24
Unit B

6. Referring to **Diagram 25**, lay out four A units, one B unit, and four light green print 5" squares in three rows. Join pieces in each row. Press seams toward squares. Join rows to make a Double Nine-Patch block. Press seams in one direction. The block should be 14" square including seam allowances. Repeat to make five Double Nine-Patch blocks total.

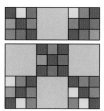

Diagram 25

Assemble Quilt Center

Referring to photo *below*, lay out blocks and setting squares in three rows. Sew together pieces in each row. Press seams toward setting squares. Join rows to make quilt center; press seams in one direction. The quilt center should be 41" square including seam allowances.

Add Borders

1. Cut and piece dark red print 2×42" strips to make:
- 2—2×44" inner border strips
- 2—2×41" inner border strips

2. Sew short inner border strips to opposite edges of quilt center. Add long inner border strips to remaining edges. Press all seams toward inner border.

3. Cut and piece red tone-on-tone 5×42" strips to make:
- 2—5×53" outer border strips
- 2—5×44" outer border strips

4. Sew short outer border strips to opposite edges of quilt center. Add long outer border strips to remaining edges to complete quilt top. Press all seams toward outer border.

Finish Quilt

1. Layer quilt top, batting, and backing; baste. (For details, see Complete the Quilt, *page 159.*)

2. Quilt as desired. The featured quilt is stitched with an allover feather design.

3. Bind with red-and-black print binding strips. (For details, see Complete the Quilt.)

ADIRONDACK BLANKET

Create a classic by joining high-contrast strips against a neutral background.

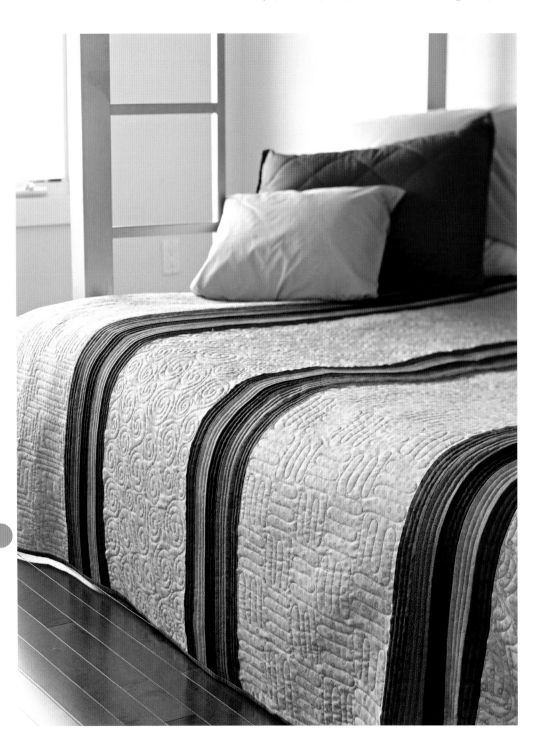

Materials

- ⅝ yard *each* red, gold, and green prints or tone-on-tones (stripe units)
- 1¼ yards blue tone-on-tone (stripe units, binding)
- ⅔ yard navy blue tone-on-tone (stripe units)
- 4½ yards beige print (background)
- 7¼ yards backing fabric
- 86×98" batting

Finished quilt: 80×92"

Cut Fabrics

Cut pieces in the following order. Cut beige print rectangles lengthwise (parallel to the selvages).

From *each* red, gold, and green print or tone-on-tone, cut:
- 8—2×42" strips

From blue tone-on-tone, cut:
- 9—2½×42" binding strips
- 8—2×42" strips

From navy blue tone-on-tone, cut:
- 10—2×42" strips

From beige print, cut:
- 2—17×80" rectangles
- 2—14×80" rectangles

Assemble Stripe Units

1. Cut and piece red, gold, green, blue, and navy blue print or tone-on-tone 2×42" strips to make:

- 4—2×80" red strips
- 4—2×80" gold strips
- 4—2×80" green strips
- 4—2×80" blue strips
- 5—2×80" navy strips

2. Referring to **Diagram 26**, sew together one 2×80" strip in each color to make an inner stripe unit. Press seams in one direction. The inner stripe unit should be 8×80" including seam allowances. Repeat to make three inner stripe units total.

Diagram 26

3. Join one *each* of navy blue, blue, and green print or tone-on-tone 2×80" strips to make a top stripe unit **(Diagram 27)**. Press seams in one direction. The top stripe unit should be 5×80" including seam allowances.

Diagram 27

4. Sew together one *each* of red, gold, and navy blue print or tone-on-tone 2×80" strips to make a bottom stripe unit **(Diagram 28)**. Press seams in one direction. The bottom stripe unit should be 5×80" including seam allowances.

Diagram 28

Assemble Quilt Top

Referring to photo *below,* lay out stripe units and beige print rectangles in nine rows, alternating 14"- and 17"-wide rectangles. Join rows to make quilt top. Press seams in one direction.

Finish Quilt

1. Layer quilt top, batting, and backing; baste. (For details, see Complete the Quilt, *page 159*.)

2. Quilt as desired. The featured quilt is stitched with horizontal parallel lines in the stripe units. Each beige print section is quilted with a different design, showcasing squares, swirls, zigzags, and fan motifs.

3. Bind with blue tone-on-tone binding strips. (For details, see Complete the Quilt.)

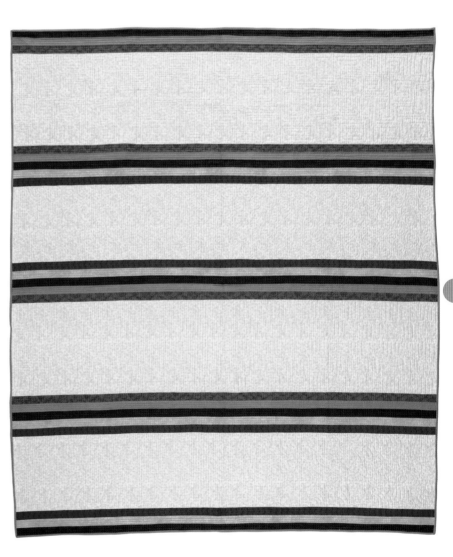

Irish Cabins

Pierre

A 1930s cream-and-Cheddar yellow quilt from the collection of Miriam Kujac has distinctive Feathered Star blocks and a whimsical Ice Cream Cone border.

Materials

4 yards solid cream (blocks, sashing, outer border, binding)

4⅞ yards solid gold (blocks, sashing, inner and outer borders)

5⅛ yards backing fabric

78×92" batting

Finished quilt: 71⅜×85⅞"
Finished block: 15⅜" square

Quantities are for 44/45"-wide, 100% cotton fabrics. Measurements include ¼" seam allowances. Sew with right sides together unless otherwise stated.

Historical Notes

The Pierre block, which appeared in the publication *Hearth and Home*, is a distinctive version of a Feathered Star. Unlike most Feathered Star blocks, the star points in a Pierre block are cut off rather than ending with a parallelogram-shape piece.

Also note the reverse placement of the lights and darks in the triangle-squares that make up the "feathers" on the Pierre block versus more common versions of Feathered Star blocks.

Cut Fabrics

Cut pieces in the following order. Cut inner border strips lengthwise (parallel to the selvages). Patterns are on *Pattern Sheet 1*. To make templates of patterns, see Make and Use Templates, *page 155*. Be sure to transfer dots marked on patterns to templates, then to fabric pieces. These dots are matching points used when joining pieces.

From solid cream, cut:
- 1—12×42" rectangle, cutting it into enough 1¼"-wide bias strips to total 360" for binding (For details, see Cutting Bias Strips, *page 155*.)
- 12—7⅛" squares, cutting each diagonally twice in an X for 48 large triangles total
- 12—6⅞" squares
- 6—5" sashing squares
- 95 of Pattern A
- 1 *each* of patterns C and C reversed
- 48—3⅞" squares
- 288—2" squares
- 96—1⅝" squares

From solid gold, cut:
- 2—5×82½" inner border strips
- 1—5×55⅝" inner border strip
- 1—3×55⅝" inner border strip
- 17—5×15⅞" sashing rectangles
- 48—4⅛" squares, cutting each in half diagonally for 96 medium triangles total
- 100 of Pattern B

continued

*"My heart leapt when I saw this perfect quilt
lying forgotten in an antiques store."*

–quilt collector Miriam Kujac

Pierre

- 288—2" squares
- 48—2" squares, cutting each in half diagonally for 96 small triangles total

Assemble Bear's Paw Units

1. Use a pencil to mark a diagonal line on wrong side of each solid cream 2" square.

2. Layer each marked solid cream 2" square atop a solid gold 2" square. Sew together each pair with two seams, stitching ¼" on each side of drawn line **(Diagram 1).**

To save time, chain-piece layered squares. To chain-piece, machine-sew pairs together one after the other without lifting presser foot or clipping

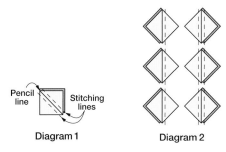

Diagram 6   Diagram 7

Diagram 1   Diagram 2

threads between pairs. First sew along one side of drawn lines, then turn group of pairs around and sew along other side of lines (**Diagram 2**). Remove chain-pieced pairs from sewing machine and clip connecting threads.

3. Cut a pair apart on drawn line to make two triangle units (**Diagram 3**). Press each triangle unit open to make two triangle-squares (**Diagram 4**). Each triangle-square should be 1⅝" square including seam allowances. Repeat with remaining pairs to make 576 triangle-squares total.

Diagram 3   Diagram 4   Diagram 5

4. Referring to **Diagram 5**, join six triangle-squares, a solid cream 3⅞" square, and a solid cream 1⅝" square in sections. Press seams in one direction. Join sections to make a Bear's Paw unit. The Bear's Paw unit should be 5" square including seam allowances. Repeat to make 48 Bear's Paw units total.

Assemble Pierre Blocks

1. Referring to **Diagram 6**, lay out three triangle-squares and one solid gold small triangle in a row. Sew together pieces; press seams in one direction. Add pieced row to right-hand edge of a solid cream large triangle. Point of solid gold small triangle will extend past edge of solid cream large triangle.

2. Join one solid gold small triangle, three triangle-squares, and one solid cream 1⅝" square in a row; press seams in one direction (**Diagram 6**). Join pieced row to left-hand edge of the solid cream large triangle. Press seams toward large triangle. Trim points of solid gold small triangles even with solid cream large triangle (**Diagram 7**).

3. Referring to **Diagram 8**, sew two solid gold medium triangles to Step 2 unit to make a star point unit. Press seams toward solid gold triangles. The star point unit should be 5×6⅞" including seam allowances.

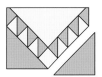

Diagram 8

4. Repeat steps 1 through 3 to make 48 star point units total.

5. Referring to **Diagram 9**, lay out four Bear's Paw units, four star point units, and one solid cream 6⅞" square in three rows. Sew together pieces in each row. Press seams in one direction, alternating direction with each row. Join rows to make a Pierre block; press seams in one direction. The block should be 15⅞" square including seam allowances. Repeat to make 12 Pierre blocks total.

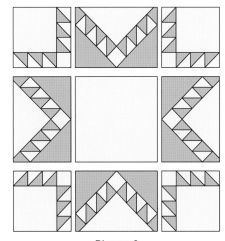

Diagram 9

continued

Quilt Assembly Diagram

Assemble Quilt Center

1. Referring to **Quilt Assembly Diagram**, lay out blocks, solid gold sashing rectangles, and solid cream sashing squares in seven horizontal rows.

2. Sew together pieces in each row. Press seams toward sashing rectangles. Join rows to make quilt center; press seams toward sashing. The quilt center should be 55⅝×75½" including seam allowances.

Assemble and Add Borders

1. Sew solid gold 3×55⅝" inner border strip to top edge of quilt center. Join solid gold 5×55⅝" inner border strip to bottom edge of quilt center. Press seams toward inner border.

2. Sew solid gold 5×82½" inner border strips to side edges of quilt center. Press seams toward inner border. The quilt center should now be 64⅜×82½" including seam allowances.

3. Referring to **Quilt Assembly Diagram**, sew together 27 solid cream A triangles and 28 solid gold B cones in a row, beginning and ending seams at dots, to make bottom outer border strip. Press seams toward solid gold pieces. Sew bottom outer border strip to bottom edge of quilt center, beginning and ending seams ¼" from edges. Press seam toward inner border.

4. Referring to **Quilt Assembly Diagram**, sew together 34 solid cream A triangles, the solid cream C triangle, and 36 solid gold B cones in a row, beginning and ending seams at dots, to make left-hand outer border strip. Press seams as before.

5. Repeat Step 4 using solid cream C reversed triangle to make right-hand outer border strip.

6. Sew outer border strips to corresponding edges of quilt center, setting in bottom corners, to complete quilt top. (For details, see Setting in Pieces, *page 157*.) Press seams toward inner border.

Finish Quilt

1. Layer quilt top, batting, and backing; baste. (For details, see Complete the Quilt, *page 159*.) Quilt as desired.

2. Join solid cream 1¼"-wide bias strips to make one continuous binding strip. Cut one end of binding strip diagonally; fold under raw edge. Beginning at top of one scallop, place binding strip against right side of quilt top, aligning binding strip's raw edge with quilt top's raw edge. Sew through all layers, stopping at point of first V between two scallops. With needle down, lift presser foot. Pivot layers to stitch binding to next scallop, using point of a seam ripper to make binding lie flat. Binding will be pulled tightly around V, so be careful not to create any folds or pleats.

Continue sewing in this manner around quilt top, ending with a small diagonal overlap of binding. Carefully trim batting and backing fabric even with quilt top edges.

3. Fold binding under ¼" and turn folded edge to back. Hand-stitch binding to backing fabric, covering machine stitching.

To make miters at each V, hand-stitch up to a V and work binding's inside corners around to create a small pleat on each side. (Use blunt end of a needle to form each pleat; there is no need to clip quilt at Vs. Take a stitch or two in fold to secure it. Stitch binding in place up to next V. Finish each V in same manner.)

optional colors

Romantic Lead

When designing her table-topper version of *Pierre,* quilt tester Laura Boehnke took her cue from the rich colors of a romantic floral collection.

"In contrast to the original quilt's pair of solid fabrics, I wanted to add visual texture by incorporating tone-on-tone, small-scale, and large-scale prints with different shades of green and red," Laura says. "I also included a bit of tan to enhance the rich, gently aged look of this piece."

SINGLE-BLOCK TABLE TOPPER

Try your hand at a new technique making this one-block beauty.

Materials

⅓ yard mottled green (block, inner border)

¼ yard green check (block)

¼ yard peach dot (block)

¾ yard blue floral (block, borders)

⅜ yard orange print (outer border)

½ yard blue print (binding)

1 yard backing fabric

36" square batting

Finished quilt: 30" square

Cut Fabrics

Cut pieces in the following order. This project uses *Pierre* patterns on *Pattern Sheet 1.*

From mottled green, cut:
- 4—5" squares
- 24—2" squares
- 4—2" squares, cutting each in half diagonally for 8 small triangles total

From green check, cut:
- 24—2" squares
- 8—1⅝" squares

From peach dot, cut:
- 1—7⅞" square, cutting it diagonally twice in an X for 4 large triangles total
- 1—6⅞" square
- 4—3⅞" squares

From blue floral, cut:
- 4—5×15⅞" inner border strips
- 4—4⅛" squares, cutting each in half diagonally for 8 medium triangles total
- 36 of Pattern A
- 8 of Pattern B

From orange print, cut:
- 40 of Pattern A
- 4 of Pattern B

From blue print, cut:
- Enough 1¼"-wide bias strips to total 135" for binding (For details, see Cutting Bias Strips, *page 155.*)

Assemble Block

1. Referring to Assemble Bear's Paw Units, *page 22,* steps 1 through 4, use mottled green and green check 2" squares, green check 1⅝" squares, and peach dot 3⅞" squares to make four Bear's Paw units (**Diagram 10**). You will have 24 triangle-squares left over.

2. Referring to Assemble Pierre Blocks, *page 23,* steps 1 through 3, use remaining Step 1 triangle-squares, green check 1⅝" squares, mottled green small triangles, peach dot large triangles, and blue floral medium triangles to make four star point units (**Diagram 11**).

Diagram 10

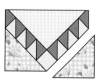

Diagram 11

3. Referring to Assemble Pierre Blocks, Step 5, join Bear's Paw units, star point units, and peach dot 6⅞" square to make a Pierre block.

Add Inner Border

1. Referring to photo *opposite*, sew blue floral inner border strips to opposite edges of block. Press seams toward inner border.

2. Add mottled green 5" squares to each end of remaining inner border strips to make inner border units; press seams toward squares. Join inner border units to remaining edges of block. Press seams toward inner border. Trim bordered block to 24¼" square including seam allowances.

Assemble and Add Outer Border

1. Referring to **Diagram 12**, sew together 10 orange print A triangles, two blue floral B cones, and nine blue floral A triangles, beginning and ending seams at dots, to make an outer border strip. Repeat to make four outer border strips total.

Diagram 12

2. Sew outer border strips to opposite edges of bordered block, beginning and ending seams ¼" from edges. Press seams toward inner border.

3. Join an orange print B cone to each end of remaining outer border strips to make outer border units. Sew outer border units to remaining edges of bordered block, setting in corners, to complete quilt top. (For details, see Setting in Pieces, *page 157*.)

Finish Quilt

1. Layer quilt top, batting, and backing; baste. (For details, see Complete the Quilt, *page 159*.)

2. Quilt as desired. Machine-quilter Mary Pepper stitched whole and partial flower motifs in the peach dot pieces and mottled green squares. She outline-quilted the blue floral pieces in the block and outer border.

3. Referring to Finish Quilt, steps 2 and 3, *page 25*, bind with blue print bias binding strips.

FOUR-BLOCK WALL HANGING

Warm colors radiate in and around

the matching pairs of stars.

Materials

⅓ yard tan print (blocks)

⅝ yard pink print (blocks, binding)

⅜ yard green print (blocks)

1 yard multicolor print (blocks, outer border)

½ yard gold print (blocks, inner border)

2⅝ yards backing fabric

46" square batting

Finished quilt: 39¼" square

Cut Fabrics

Cut pieces in the following order.

From tan print, cut:
- 48—2" squares
- 16—1⅝" squares

From pink print, cut:
- 4—2½×42" binding strips
- 48—2" squares
- 8—2" squares, cutting each in half diagonally for 16 small triangles total

From green print, cut:
- 2—7⅛" squares, cutting each diagonally twice in an X for 8 large triangles total
- 2—6⅞" squares
- 8—3⅞" squares

From multicolor print, cut:
- 2—3½×39¼" outer border strips
- 2—3½×33¼" outer border strips
- 2—7⅛" squares, cutting each diagonally twice in an X for 8 large triangles total
- 2—6⅞" squares
- 8—4⅛" squares, cutting each in half diagonally for 16 medium triangles total
- 8—3⅞" squares

From gold print, cut:
- 2—1½×33¼" inner border strips
- 2—1½×31¼" inner border strips
- 8—4⅛" squares, cutting each in half diagonally for 16 medium triangles total
- 48—2" squares
- 8—2" squares, cutting each in half diagonally for 16 small triangles total

Assemble Blocks

1. Referring to Assemble Bear's Paw Units, *page 22*, steps 1 through 4, use tan and pink print 2" squares, tan print 1⅝" squares, and green print 3⅞" squares to make eight Bear's Paw units **(Diagram 13)**. You will have 48 triangle-squares left over.

2. Referring to Assemble Pierre Blocks, *page 23*, steps 1 through 3, use remaining Step 1 triangle-squares, tan print 1⅝" squares, pink print small triangles, green print large triangles, and multicolor print medium triangles to make eight star point units **(Diagram 14)**.

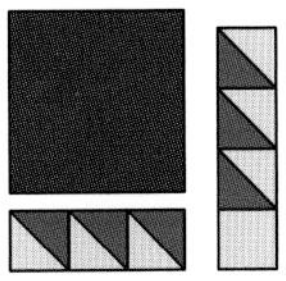

Diagram 13

Diagram 14

3. Referring to Assemble Pierre Blocks, Step 5, and photo *opposite*, join four Bear's Paw units, four star point units, and a green print 6⅞" square to make a green-and-pink Pierre block. Repeat to make a second green-and-pink Pierre block.

4. Repeat steps 1 through 3 to make two gold Pierre blocks, substituting gold print pieces for the pink print, multicolor print pieces for the green print, and gold print medium triangles for the multicolor print.

Assemble Quilt Center

Referring to photo, sew together blocks in pairs. Press seams in opposite directions. Join pairs to make quilt center; press seam in one direction. The quilt center should be 31¼" square including seam allowances.

Add Borders

1. Sew short inner border strips to opposite edges of quilt center. Add long inner border strips to remaining edges. Press all seams toward inner border.

2. Sew short outer border strips to opposite edges of quilt center. Add long outer border strips to remaining edges to complete quilt top. Press all seams toward outer border.

Finish Quilt

1. Layer quilt top, batting, and backing; baste. (For details, see Complete the Quilt, *page 159*.)

2. Quilt as desired. The featured quilt is stitched with a feather motif in each block center and large triangle, curved triangles in the star points, and radiating lines in block corners. A wave design is quilted in the inner border, and swirls are stitched in the outer border.

3. Bind with pink print binding strips. (For details, see Complete the Quilt.)

Starry Night

Straight-set, pieced blocks form distinct stars

on this striking two-color antique quilt.

Materials

4¼ yards solid pink (blocks, binding)

5¾ yards solid black (blocks)

4⅛ yards backing fabric

73×84" batting

Finished quilt: 66½×77½"
Finished block: 5½" square
For additional quilt sizes, see Optional Sizes chart on Pattern Sheet 2.

Quantities are for 44/45"-wide, 100% cotton fabrics. Measurements include ¼" seam allowances. Sew with right sides together unless otherwise stated.

Cut Fabrics

Cut pieces in the following order. Patterns are on *Pattern Sheet 1*. To make templates of patterns, see Make and Use Templates, *page 155.* Be sure to transfer dots marked on patterns to templates, then to fabric pieces. These dots are matching points used when joining pieces.

From solid pink, cut:
- 8—2½×42" binding strips
- 672 of Pattern A

From solid black, cut:
- 672 of Pattern B

Assemble Starry Night Blocks

1. Layer a solid pink A piece atop a solid black B piece, carefully aligning dots where the ¼" seam allowances intersect **(Diagram 1)**. Pin at each dot, then pin between dots.

Diagram 1

2. Join pieces, sewing from edge to edge, to make a unit. Be careful to not stretch the bias edges as you sew. Press seam open. Repeat to make four units total.

continued

Starry Night

3. Sew together the units in pairs (**Diagram 2**). Press seams open. Join pairs to complete a Starry Night block. Press seam open. The block should be 6" square including seam allowances.

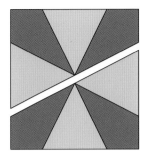

Diagram 2

4. Repeat steps 1 through 3 to make 168 Starry Night blocks total.

Assemble Quilt Top

1. Referring to photo *opposite,* lay out blocks in 14 horizontal rows.

2. Sew together blocks in each row. Press seams in one direction, alternating direction with each row. Join rows to complete quilt top. Press seams in one direction.

Finish Quilt

1. Layer quilt top, batting, and backing; baste. (For details, see Complete the Quilt, *page 159.)*

2. Quilt as desired. The quilter of this antique hand-quilted ¼" inside each piece.

3. Bind with solid pink binding strips. (For details, see Complete the Quilt.)

optional colors

Lasso the Stars

Quilt tester Laura Boehnke added Western flair to her interpretation of *Starry Night* with cowboy-theme novelty prints in bright colors.

"I carefully planned my fabric placement so that the corners of my blocks create stars of matching fabrics and a checkerboard pattern emerges in the background," Laura says.

"I also added a border to make my version into a finished wall hanging for a room where a child dreams of riding off into the sunset."

PATRIOTIC PATCHWORK QUILT

Salute Old Glory with an all-American wall hanging.

Starry Night

Materials

12—¼-yard pieces assorted beige-and-red prints (blocks)

12—¼-yard pieces assorted red prints (blocks)

½ yard total assorted blue prints (blocks)

6—¼-yard pieces assorted cream-and-blue prints (blocks)

½ yard tan print (binding)

1¾ yards backing fabric

62×40" batting

Finished quilt: 55½×33½"

Cut Fabrics

Cut pieces in the following order. This project uses *Starry Night* patterns on *Pattern Sheet 1.*

Although this quilt is scrappy, the prints used in each block are carefully planned to match surrounding blocks. In each red block, there are two different red prints, creating rows of matching red star points when blocks are joined; each beige-and-red triangle matches a print in a neighboring block, forming matching beige-and-red diamonds. In the blue blocks, blue prints are used randomly, while cream-and-blue prints are placed to create stars of matching prints where the blocks intersect.

To achieve a similar look, use a design wall or other flat surface to lay out the pieces for 48 red blocks and 12 blue blocks. When you are pleased with the arrangement, remove and stitch the pieces for one block at a time.

From *each* of six assorted beige-and-red prints, cut:
• 20 of Pattern A for long red block rows
From *each* of six remaining assorted beige-and-red prints, cut:
• 12 of Pattern A for short red block rows
From *each* of six assorted red prints, cut:
• 20 of Pattern B for long red block rows
From *each* of six remaining assorted red prints, cut:
• 12 of Pattern B for short red block rows
From assorted blue prints, cut:
• 48 of Pattern A
From *each* assorted cream-and-blue print, cut:
• 8 of Pattern B
From tan print, cut:
• 5—2½×42" binding strips

Assemble Blocks

1. Referring to Assemble Starry Night Blocks, *page 31,* steps 1 through 3, use beige-and-red print A pieces and red print B pieces to make 48 red Starry Night blocks (**Diagram 3**).

2. Using blue print A pieces and cream-and-blue print B pieces, repeat Step 1 to make 12 blue Starry Night blocks (**Diagram 4**).

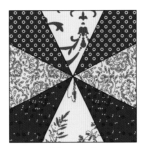   

Diagram 3   Diagram 4

Assemble Quilt Top

Referring to photo *opposite,* lay out blocks in six rows. Sew together blocks in each row. Press seams in one direction, alternating direction with each row. Join rows to make quilt top. Press seams in one direction.

Finish Quilt

1. Layer quilt top, batting, and backing; baste. (For details, see Complete the Quilt, *page 159.*)

2. Quilt as desired. On the featured quilt, the blue section is outline-quilted inside the cream stars at block intersections, and the background is stitched with a continuous stipple. The red rows are quilted with horizontal wavy lines.

3. Bind with tan print binding strips. (For details, see Complete the Quilt.)

PRETTY PIPED PILLOW

A little time to make a few blocks? Turn them into a pillow.

Materials

½ yard total assorted green, red, blue, and brown prints (blocks)

⅓ yard total assorted tan prints (blocks)

¼ yard total assorted cream prints (blocks)

⅞ yard red-and-black print (piping, pillow back)

23" square muslin (lining)

23" square batting

2 yards ½"-diameter cording

Large safety pin

16"-square pillow form

Finished pillow: 17½" square

Cut Fabrics

Cut pieces in the following order. This project uses *Starry Night* patterns on *Pattern Sheet 1*.

From assorted green prints, cut:
• 10 of Pattern B

From assorted red prints, cut:
• 9 of Pattern B

From assorted blue prints, cut:
• 9 of Pattern B

From assorted brown prints, cut:
• 8 of Pattern B

From assorted tan prints, cut:
• 20 of Pattern A (5 sets of 4 matching triangles)

From assorted cream prints, cut:
- 16 of Pattern A (4 sets of 4 matching triangles)

From red-and-black print, cut:
- 4—2½×42" strips for piping
- 2—19×17" rectangles

Assemble Pillow Top

1. Referring to Assemble Starry Night Blocks, *page 31*, steps 1 through 3, and the **Pillow Assembly Diagram** for color placement, use assorted green, red, blue, and brown print B pieces and sets of matching tan print A pieces to make five tan Starry Night blocks.

Pillow Assembly Diagram

2. Substituting cream prints for the tan prints, repeat Step 1 to make four cream Starry Night blocks.

3. Sew together blocks in three rows, alternating tan and cream blocks. Press seams in one direction, alternating direction with each row. Join rows to complete pillow top; press seams in one direction. The pillow top should be 17" square including seam allowances.

Finish Pillow

1. Layer pillow top, batting, and muslin lining; baste. (For details, see Complete the Quilt, *page 159.*)

2. Quilt as desired. The featured pillow top is outline-quilted ⅛" inside each tan and cream print triangle.

3. Cut and piece red-and-black print 2½×42" strips to make a 145"-long strip. Fold under 1" at one short end of strip; press. With wrong side inside,

fold strip in half lengthwise; press. Using a ¼" seam allowance, sew together long edges to make a piping cover.

4. Attach a large safety pin to one end of ½"-diameter cording; insert pin into folded end of piping cover. Push cording into piping cover, moving safety pin a short distance at a time and forming gathers in piping cover (**Diagram 5**). Continue gathering until entire length of cording is enclosed in piping cover. Arrange gathers evenly along length of cord to make piping.

Diagram 5

5. Aligning raw edges and using a machine zipper foot, stitch piping to right side of pillow top. (For details, see Covered Cording, steps 2 and 3, on *Pattern Sheet 2.*)

6. With wrong side inside, fold each red-and-black print 19×17" rectangle in half to make two 9½×17" double-thick pillow back rectangles.

7. Overlap folded edges of pillow back rectangles about 2" to make a 17"-square pillow back (**Diagram 6**). Baste along top and bottom edges.

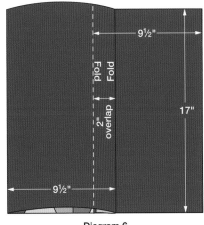

Diagram 6

8. With right sides together, layer pillow top and pillow back; pin or baste edges. Sew together through all layers to make pillow cover, rounding corners slightly.

9. Turn pillow cover right side out through opening in pillow back. Insert 16"-square pillow form.

ROUND ABOUT

The geometry of quilting most often results in blocks comprised of straight lines and eye-catching sharp angles. Perhaps that's why circles, when they appear, always stand out on quilt designs.

Some think curved edges are difficult to sew, but the techniques that follow prove differently. What's certain is this: The fluid motion and graceful arcs found in designs that go round and round make for stunningly beautiful quilts.

50

40

47

60

Mesmerize

Clear colors swirl in six-piece blocks across this bright

wall hanging by designer Tammy Kelly.

Materials

3½ yards total assorted pink and fuchsia prints (blocks)

3½ yards total assorted blue and purple prints (blocks)

2⅓ yards total assorted green prints (blocks)

⅝ yard mottled pink print (binding)

4 yards backing fabric

72" square batting

Finished quilt: 66" square
Finished block: 6" square

Quantities are for 44/45"-wide, 100% cotton fabrics. Measurements include ¼" seam allowances. Sew with right sides together unless otherwise stated.

Cut Fabrics

Cut pieces in the following order. Patterns are on *Pattern Sheet 1*. To make templates of patterns, see Make and Use Templates, *page 155*.

Designer Notes

Tammy Kelly adapted *Mesmerize* from an antique quilt known as *New Moon*.

"The late-1800s version was in tans, reds, and blues," Tammy says. "I chose to bring it into the 21st century with batiks."

From assorted pink and fuchsia prints, cut:
• 49—6⅞" squares, cutting each in half diagonally for 98 triangles total
• 168 of Pattern B (42 sets of 4 matching pieces)

From assorted blue and purple prints, cut:
• 44—6⅞" squares, cutting each in half diagonally for 88 triangles total
• 192 of Pattern B (48 sets of 4 matching pieces)

From assorted green prints, cut:
• 28—6⅞" squares, cutting each in half diagonally for 56 triangles total
• 128 of Pattern B (32 sets of 4 matching pieces)

From mottled pink print, cut:
• 7—2½×42" binding strips

Assemble Block Centers

1. Sew together two assorted pink or fuchsia print triangles to make a pink triangle-square (**Diagram 1**). Press seam toward darker triangle. The triangle-square should be 6½" square including seam allowances.

Diagram 1

2. Repeat Step 1 with remaining pink and fuchsia print triangles to make 49 pink triangle-squares total.

continued

3. Repeat Step 1 with assorted blue and purple print triangles to make 44 blue triangle-squares total.

4. Repeat Step 1 with assorted green print triangles to make 28 green triangle-squares total.

5. Referring to **Diagram 2**, place Pattern A template on a pink triangle-square and trace curved edges; cut on marked lines to make a pink block center. Repeat to make 49 pink block centers total.

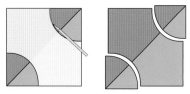

Diagram 2

6. Repeat Step 5 with blue and green triangle-squares to make 44 blue block centers and 28 green block centers total.

Assemble Block Corners

The following instructions result in four matching block corners (one set). Repeat the instructions to make 61 sets of block corners total—21 pink sets, 24 blue sets, and 16 green sets.

1. Gather four matching pink or fuchsia print B pieces and four matching pink or fuchsia print B pieces in a different print.

2. Layer B pieces in contrasting pairs, keeping same print on top in each pair. Chain-piece layered pieces to make four matching block corners (**Diagram 3**). To chain-piece, machine-sew pairs together one after the other without lifting presser foot or clipping threads between pairs. (Be sure to sew along same side of each pair so fabrics will

alternate when they are later sewn into a circle.) Press seams toward darker fabrics.

Assemble Quilt Top

The quilt top changes color in diagonal rows from upper left to lower right. Use a design wall and refer to **Quilt Assembly Diagram** to guide your placement choices.

1. Lay out pink, blue, and green block centers in 11 horizontal rows. Note direction of block center seams. Tammy arranged block centers and corners so that matching fabrics would not abut.

2. Add block corners to layout. Note that matching block corners form a circle at each intersection of four block centers and half circles along quilt's outer edges.

3. Beginning with upper left-hand block, layer a block corner on block center; place a pin at seam intersection (**Diagram 4**). Then place a pin at each end; pin generously in between, picking up only a few threads at a time, until pieces fit together smoothly (**Diagram 5**). Sew together, removing each pin just before needle reaches it; press seam toward block corner.

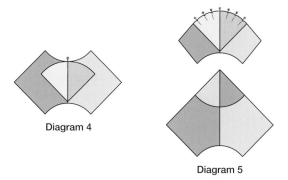

Diagram 4

Diagram 5

4. Repeat Step 3 with second block corner to make a block (**Diagram 6**). The block should be 6½" square including seam allowances.

Diagram 6

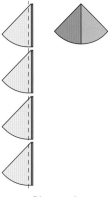

Diagram 3

5. Repeat steps 3 and 4 to make 121 blocks total. After completing each block, return it to design wall, noting direction of center seam.

6. Sew together blocks in each row. Press seams in one direction, alternating direction with each row. Join rows to complete quilt top; press seams in one direction.

Finish Quilt

1. Layer quilt top, batting, and backing; baste. (For details, see Complete the Quilt, *page 159*.)

2. Quilt as desired. Machine-quilter Linda DeVries stitched an allover swirl pattern using variegated thread.

3. Bind with mottled pink print binding strips. (For details, see Complete the Quilt.)

Quilt Assembly Diagram

optional colors

Optical Illusion

The wall hanging that quilt tester Laura Boehnke created takes *Mesmerize* on a wild ride. Her choice of geometric fabrics gives the impression that there's a whole lot of piecing going on. In reality, there are still just six pieces per block.

"I love to take graphic, geometric prints and piece them into a block like this," Laura says. "The stripes in the fabric make it appear that there are lots of tiny pieces sewn together to make the block."

RETRO APRON

Turn back the clock with a fanciful apron that's fresh, fun, and functional.

Materials

2—8" squares *each* red, blue, cream-and-red, and cream-and-blue prints (blocks)

⅞ yard red-and-blue floral (neck strap, waistband, tie, ruffle)

12½" square blue-and-red plaid (bib backing)

½ yard cream print (apron skirt)

4 yards ¾"-wide rickrack: red

Finished apron: 24½ ×31¼"
(excluding ties and strap)

Quantities are for 44/45"-wide, 100% cotton fabrics. Measurements include ¼" seam allowances. Sew with right sides together unless otherwise stated.

Cut Fabrics

Cut pieces in the following order. This project uses *Mesmerize* patterns on *Pattern Sheet 1*.

From *each* red, blue, cream-and-red, and cream-and-blue print, cut:

• 1—6⅞" square, cutting it in half diagonally for 2 triangles total (you will use 1 triangle from each print)

• 2 of Pattern B (from leftover triangles)

From red-and-blue floral, cut:
- 1—5×42" strip
- 1—5×21" strip
- 1—2½×42" strip
- 1—2½×26" strip
- 1—2½×25" strip
- 1—2½×24½" strip
- 2—2½×21" strips

From cream print, cut:
- 1—14½×42" rectangle

From red rickrack, cut:
- 1—42"-long piece
- 2—25½"-long pieces
- 1—17"-long piece
- 1—12½"-long piece

Assemble Blocks

1. Referring to Assemble Block Centers, *page 41*, Step 1, use a red print triangle and a cream-and-red print triangle to make a red triangle-square. Repeat to make a second red triangle-square.

2. Repeat Step 1 using blue print triangles and cream-and-blue print triangles to make two blue triangle-squares.

3. Referring to Assemble Block Centers, Step 5, *page 42*, use Pattern A template and triangle-squares to make four block centers.

4. Referring to Assemble Block Corners, *page 42*, Step 2, use a red print B piece and a cream-and-red print B piece to make a red block corner. Repeat to make four red block corners total.

5. Repeat Step 4 using blue print B pieces and cream-and-blue print B pieces to make four blue block corners.

6. Referring to Assemble Quilt Top, *page 42*, steps 3 and 4, use red block centers and block corners to make two red blocks **(Diagram 7)**. Repeat using blue block centers and blue block corners to make two blue blocks.

Diagram 7

Assemble Apron Bib

1. Referring to photo *opposite,* join blocks in pairs. Press seams in opposite directions. Join pairs to make bib front. Press seam in one direction. The bib front should be 12½" square including seam allowances.

2. Referring to photo, pin 17"-long rickrack on bib front in a V shape, turning rickrack on an outside curve to form bottom angle of the V. Using red thread, topstitch to bib front through center of rickrack.

3. Pin 12½"-long rickrack to right side of bib front along top edge, with curved tips of rickrack edge extending just slightly above raw fabric edge; baste.

4. With right side inside, fold red-and-blue floral 2½×26" strip in half lengthwise; press. Sew along long edge. Turn right side out to make a 1×26" neck strap; press. With raw edges aligned, baste neck strap to bib front atop rickrack, placing ends 1" away from each side edge **(Diagram 8** on *page 46*).

continued

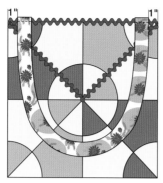

Diagram 8

5. With right sides together, layer bib front and blue-and-red plaid bib backing. Join along all edges, leaving an opening on lower edge for turning and being careful not to catch neck strap in side seams. Turn to right side and hand-stitch opening closed; press to make apron bib.

Assemble Apron Skirt and Ties

1. Join red-and-blue floral 5×42" and 5×21" strips along short edges to make a 5×62½" ruffle strip. Press seam open.

2. Turn under ¼" along one long edge of ruffle strip; press. Turn under ¼" again; press. Sew through all layers close to first folded edge to hem.

3. With a basting stitch, sew ½" from long raw edge of ruffle strip. Pull up threads to gather edge.

4. With raw edges aligned, match midpoint of gathered ruffle strip with midpoint of a long edge of cream print 14½×42" rectangle. Pin and stitch with ½" seam (**Diagram 9**). Press seam toward cream print. Topstitch ¼" from seam line to make apron skirt.

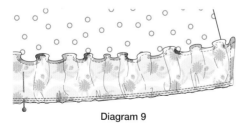

Diagram 9

5. Repeat Step 2 to hem side edges of apron skirt.

6. Using a basting stitch, sew ½" from top raw edge of apron skirt. Pull up threads to gather edge.

7. With raw edges aligned, match midpoint of gathered apron skirt with midpoint of red-and-blue floral 2½×25" waistband strip; leave a ¼" seam allowance at each end of strip (**Diagram 10**). Pin and stitch with ½" seam. Press seam toward waistband.

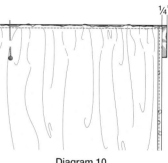

Diagram 10

8. Join a red-and-blue floral 2½×21" strip to each short edge of waistband to make tie fronts. Press seams open.

9. Sew together red-and-blue floral 2½×42" and 2½×24½" strips along short edges to make a 2½×66" tie backing strip. Press seam open.

10. With right sides together, pin tie backing strip to top edge of waistband and all edges of tie fronts. Sew together, leaving lower edge of tie backing unstitched for turning (**Diagram 11**). Stitch tie ends at a 45° angle. Trim excess fabric at tie ends, leaving a ¼" seam allowance. Turn waistband and ties right side out. Hand- or machine-stitch lower edge of tie backing to apron skirt.

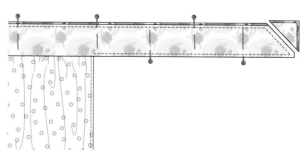

Diagram 11

Finish Apron

1. With apron bib and apron skirt right side up, pin bottom edge of apron bib to top edge of waistband, aligning midpoints and overlapping ¼" (**Diagram 12**). Sew together through all layers to make apron body.

2. Turn under ½" on each end of 42"-long rickrack; press. Pin rickrack above ruffle seam, centering it over topstitching line. Topstitch to apron skirt through center of rickrack.

3. In the same manner, fold under ends of each 25½"-long rickrack and pin to top and bottom edges of waistband. Topstitch in place to complete apron.

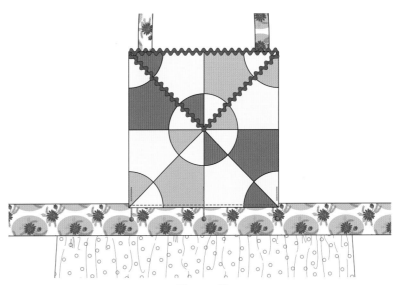

Diagram 12

ICED MOCHA BED QUILT

Just a smattering of circles simplifies the look on this quilt.

Materials

6 yards total assorted brown, tan, turquoise, light blue, and cream prints (blocks)

1½ yards mottled brown (blocks, inner border, piping)

3 yards turquoise swirl print (blocks, outer border, binding)

8⅓ yards backing fabric

100" square batting

Finished quilt: 93½" square

Cut Fabrics

Cut pieces in the following order. This project uses *Mesmerize* patterns on *Pattern Sheet 1*.

From assorted brown, tan, turquoise, light blue, and cream prints, cut:
- 155—6⅞" squares, cutting each in half diagonally for 310 triangles total
- 77 of Pattern B

From mottled brown, cut:
- 9—2½×42" strips for inner border
- 10—1×42" strips for piping

- 7—6⅞" squares, cutting each in half diagonally for 14 triangles total
- 3 of Pattern B

From turquoise swirl print, cut:
- 10—6×42" strips for outer border
- 10—2½×42" binding strips
- 7—6⅞" squares, cutting each in half diagonally for 14 triangles total
- 4 of Pattern B

Assemble Triangle-Squares and Blocks

1. Referring to Assemble Block Centers, *page 41*, Step 1, use assorted print, mottled brown, and turquoise swirl print triangles to make 169 triangle-squares.

2. Referring to Assemble Block Centers, Step 5, *page 42*, and tracing only one curved edge of the template, use Pattern A template and 42 triangle-squares to make 42 block centers (**Diagram 13**).

Diagram 13

continued

3. Referring to Assemble Block Corners, *page 42,* Step 2, use assorted print, mottled brown, and turquoise swirl print B pieces in various color combinations to make 42 block corners.

4. Referring to Assemble Quilt Top, *page 42,* Step 3, use a block center and a block corner to make a block **(Diagram 14)**. The block should be 6½" square including seam allowances. Repeat to make 42 blocks total.

Diagram 14

Assemble Quilt Center

1. Referring to photo at *right,* lay out blocks and remaining triangle-squares in 13 rows, distributing blocks as desired. To create circle and half-circle shapes, arrange some blocks so B pieces meet at block intersections.

2. Sew together pieces in each row. Press seams in one direction, alternating direction with each row. Join rows to make quilt center. Press seams in one direction. The quilt center should be 78½" square including seam allowances.

Add Borders

1. Cut and piece mottled brown 2½×42" strips to make:
- 2—2½×82½" inner border strips
- 2—2½×78½" inner border strips

2. Join short inner border strips to opposite edges of quilt center. Add long inner border strips to remaining edges. Press all seams toward inner border.

3. Cut and piece turquoise swirl print 6×42" strips to make:
- 2—6×93½" outer border strips
- 2—6×82½" outer border strips

4. Sew short outer border strips to opposite edges of quilt center. Add long outer border strips to remaining edges to complete quilt top. Press all seams toward outer border.

Finish Quilt

1. Layer quilt top, batting, and backing; baste. (For details, see Complete the Quilt, *page 159.*)

2. Quilt as desired. The featured quilt center was stitched in blue thread with an allover swirling flame design and concentric circles where block corners meet. The outer border was quilted with parallel lines.

3. Cut and piece mottled brown 1×42" strips to make:
- 4—1×93½" piping strips

4. With wrong side inside, fold each piping strip in half lengthwise; press. Aligning raw edges, baste piping strips to quilt top using a scant ¼" seam allowance.

5. Bind with turquoise swirl print binding strips. (For details, see Complete the Quilt.) (About ¼" of piping will show between quilt top and binding edge after binding is turned to back.)

Round & Round

Designer Judy Clara Blok's variation of the Wheel of Mystery block creates undulating curves and overlapping circles.

Materials
2 yards dark pink stripe (blocks)

1¾ yards cream floral (blocks, inner border)

3⅜ yards moss green floral (blocks, outer border, binding)

3½ yards backing fabric

63" square batting

Finished quilt: 57" square

Quantities are for 44/45"-wide, 100% cotton fabrics. Measurements include ¼" seam allowances. Sew with right sides together unless otherwise stated.

Cut Fabrics
Cut pieces in the following order. Patterns are on *Pattern Sheet 1.* To make templates of patterns, see Make and Use Templates, *page 155.* Be sure to transfer dots marked on patterns to templates, then to fabric pieces. These dots are matching points used when joining pieces.

From dark pink stripe, cut:
- 72 of Pattern B
- 108 of Pattern A

From cream floral, cut:
- 5—1¼×42" strips for inner border
- 72 of Pattern B
- 36 of Pattern A

From moss green floral, cut:
- 6—6×42" strips for outer border
- 6—2½×42" binding strips
- 24 *each* of patterns D and D reversed
- 48 of Pattern E
- 72 of Pattern C
- 4—3" squares
- 8—2×3" rectangles
- 4—2" squares

Assemble Blocks
I. Layer a dark pink stripe B piece atop a dark pink stripe A piece; match center marks on curved edges **(Diagram 1)**. Using slender pins and picking up only a few fabric threads, pin at center, then at each end; pin generously in between **(Diagram 2)**. Sew together pieces, removing each pin just before needle reaches it, to make a pink AB unit **(Diagram 3)**. Press seam toward B piece. Repeat to make 36 pink AB units total.

Diagram 1   Diagram 2   Diagram 3

continued

2. Referring to Step 1 and **Diagram 4**, use cream floral B pieces and dark pink stripe A pieces to make 72 cream-and-pink AB units.

3. Referring to Step 1 and **Diagram 5**, use dark pink stripe B pieces and cream floral A pieces to make 36 pink-and-cream AB units.

Diagram 4   Diagram 5

4. Sew a pink AB unit to curved edge of a moss green floral C piece **(Diagram 6)**. Add a second pink AB unit to remaining curved edge to make a pink ABC unit **(Diagram 7)**. Press seams toward AB units. Repeat to make 18 pink ABC units total.

Diagram 6   Diagram 7

5. Referring to Step 4 and **Diagram 8**, use cream-and-pink AB units and moss green floral C pieces to make 36 cream-and-pink ABC units.

6. In same manner, add pink-and-cream AB units to curved edges of a moss green floral E piece to make a pink-and-cream ABE unit **(Diagram 9)**. Press seams toward AB units. Repeat to make 16 pink-and-cream ABE units total.

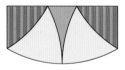
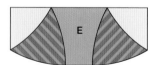

Diagram 8   Diagram 9

7. Referring to **Diagram 10**, sew together two moss green floral C pieces to make a CC unit. Press seam open. Repeat to make nine CC units total.

Diagram 10

8. Add a pink ABC unit to each curved edge of a CC unit to make block 1 **(Diagram 11)**. Press seams in one direction. Block 1 should be 6½" square including seam allowances. Repeat to make nine total of block 1.

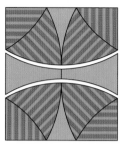

Diagram 11

9. Referring to **Diagram 12**, sew together two moss green floral E pieces to make a short EE unit. Press seam open. Repeat to make 12 short EE units total.

Diagram 12

10. Add a cream-and-pink ABC unit to each curved edge of a short EE unit to make block 2 **(Diagram 13)**. Press seams in one direction. Block 2 should be 6½×8" including seam allowances. Repeat to make 12 total of block 2.

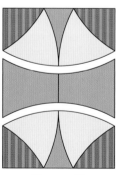

Diagram 13

11. Referring to **Diagram 14**, sew together two moss green floral E pieces and one moss green floral 2" square to make a long EE unit. Press seams toward square. Repeat to make four long EE units total.

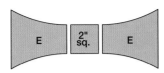

Diagram 14

12. Add a pink-and-cream ABE unit to each curved edge of a long EE unit to make block 3 (**Diagram 15**). Press seams in one direction. Block 3 should be 8" square including seam allowances. Repeat to make four total of block 3.

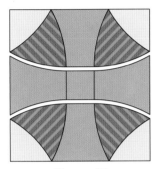

Diagram 15

13. Join a moss green floral D and D reversed piece to make a short DD unit (**Diagram 16**). Press seam open. Repeat to make 12 short DD units total.

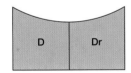

Diagram 16

14. Sew together a cream-and-pink ABC unit and a short DD unit to make block 4 (**Diagram 17**). Press seam in one direction. Block 4 should be 6½×6" including seam allowances. Repeat to make 12 total of block 4.

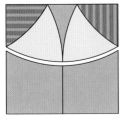

Diagram 17

15. Referring to **Diagram 18**, sew together a moss green floral D piece, 2×3" rectangle, and D reversed piece to make a long DD unit. Press seams toward rectangle. Repeat to make eight long DD units total.

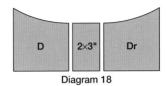

Diagram 18

16. Sew together a pink-and-cream ABE unit and a long DD unit to make block 5 (**Diagram 19** on *page 54*). Press seam in one direction. Block 5 should be 8×6" including seam allowances. Repeat to make eight total of block 5.

continued

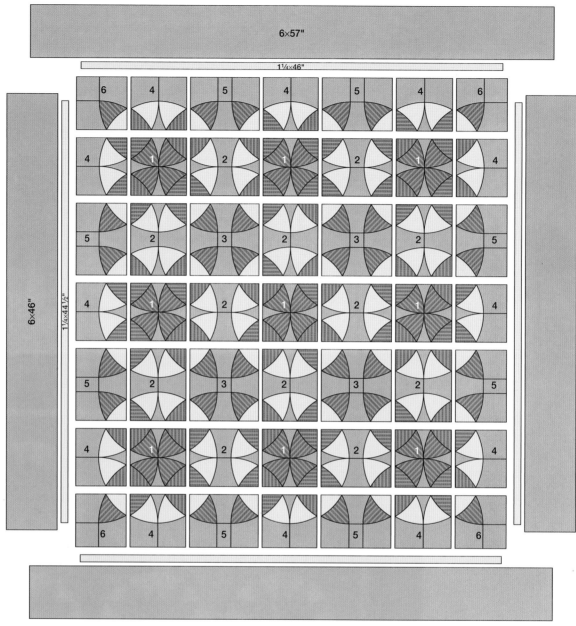

6×57"

1¼×46"

6×46"

1¼×44½"

Quilt Assembly Diagram

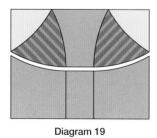

Diagram 19

Press seams in opposite directions. Join rows to make block 6. Press seam in one direction. Block 6 should be 6" square including seam allowances. Repeat to make four total of block 6.

17. Lay out a moss green floral D piece, a pink-and-cream AB unit, a moss green floral 3" square, and a moss green floral D reversed piece in two rows (**Diagram 20**). Sew together pieces in each row.

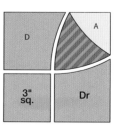

Diagram 20

Assemble Quilt Center

1. Referring to **Quilt Assembly Diagram**, lay out blocks 1 through 6 in seven horizontal rows.

2. Sew together blocks in each row. Press seams in one direction, alternating direction with each row. Join rows to make quilt center. Press seams in one direction. The quilt center should be 44½" square including seam allowances.

Add Borders

1. Cut and piece cream print 1¼×42" strips to make:
- 2—1¼×46" inner border strips
- 2—1¼×44½" inner border strips

2. Sew short inner border strips to opposite edges of quilt center. Join long inner border strips to remaining edges. Press all seams toward inner border.

3. Cut and piece moss green floral 6×42" strips to make:
- 2—6×57" outer border strips
- 2—6×46" outer border strips

4. Sew short outer border strips to opposite edges of quilt center. Join long outer border strips to remaining edges to complete quilt top. Press all seams toward outer border.

Finish Quilt

1. Layer quilt top, batting, and backing; baste. (For details, see Complete the Quilt, *page 159.*)

2. Quilt as desired. Designer Judy Clara Blok stitched in the ditch of the inner border and machine-quilted a 2" diagonal grid in the outer border. She outline-quilted each piece of the quilt center **(Quilting Diagram).**

3. Bind with moss green floral binding strips. (For details, see Complete the Quilt.)

Quilting Diagram

optional colors

Rings of Gold

Gold-etched paisley prints dress up quilt tester Laura Boehnke's elegant table runner. "I used three different prints in place of the original quilt's dark pink stripe," Laura says. "Breaking up the blocks like this draws attention to the lovely small-scale details of the fabric." The end result is a black, gold, and bronze kaleidoscope with a hint of Asian design.

COLOR IT YOUR OWN

Use the following illustrations as a color springboard when designing your next quilt.

Color is often the first thing that attracts us to a quilt. Whether the hues are soft and subtle or bold and bright, the quiltmaker's color choices express the mood of the quilt.

The easiest way to create a quilt that reflects your personality is to begin by choosing fabrics in colors you like. Keep the contrast, color variations, and character of your prints in mind as you make your selections. Understanding the basics of these three elements and how they interact is helpful.

Contrast, or value, is an objective quality most often expressed in terms of light, medium, or dark fabrics. Color, or hue, is more subjective and often evokes emotion, sometimes being described in terms of warm or cool colors. The character of the fabrics refers to the features that change how each one works in a block or an overall quilt top. Prints can vary from elegant florals to reproductions to novelty prints or stripes, with each having its own character.

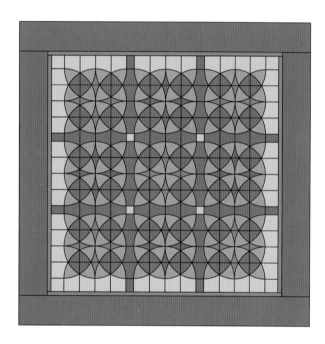

The **horizontal and vertical grid** comes to the forefront of this design, and the circles appear to recede. A closer look reveals a hidden treasure—violet stars in five of the circle centers.

Careful color placement can create primary and secondary designs. Here the pink circles seemingly pop off the quilt center. A secondary purple cross design also emerges from the center. A design wall is great for auditioning color placement when laying out quilts.

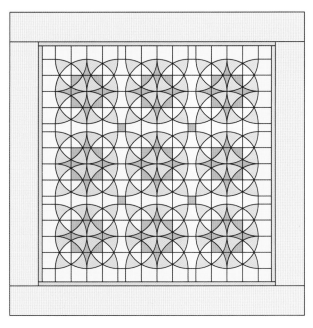

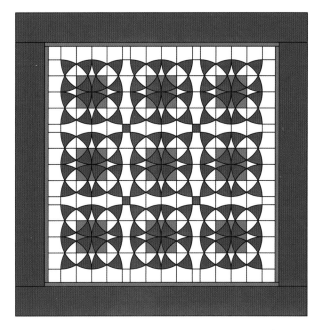

Blue and orange are complementary colors, opposite one another on the color wheel. A small amount of a color's complement, such as adding a dash of orange to the quilt center, *above,* can serve as a nice accent.

Blue block centers bring an angular focus to this variation, providing a juxtaposition to the curves in the two-color, red-and-white circles.

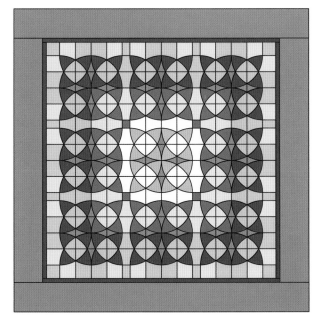

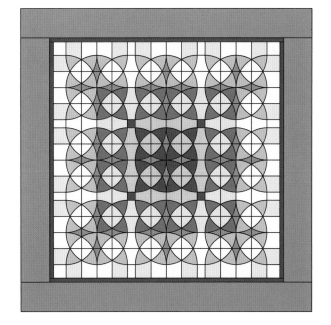

Light, medium, and dark hues of the same colors create a luminescence when carefully placed to radiate from the quilt center.

Reversing the placement of the same colors used at *left* creates a quilt with an opposite effect. Here, the center appears to have more depth than the surrounding outer circles.

BLOWING DANDELIONS
WALL HANGING

Mix soft pastels with bright white to create an altogether different swirling pattern.

Materials

½ yard green print (blocks, binding)

⅓ yard yellow print (blocks)

⅓ yard gold polka dot (blocks)

⅓ yard solid white (blocks)

½ yard light green polka dot (blocks)

⅓ yard light green print (inner border)

⅔ yard green stripe (outer border)

1 yard backing fabric

36" square batting

Finished quilt: 30" square

Cut Fabrics

Cut pieces in the following order. This project uses *Round & Round* patterns on *Pattern Sheet 1*.

From green print, cut:
- 3—2½×42" binding strips
- 16 of Pattern A
- 4 of Pattern B
- 1—2" square

From yellow print, cut:
- 16 of Pattern B

From gold polka dot, cut:
- 16 of Pattern A

From solid white, cut:
- 4 of Pattern A
- 16 of Pattern B

From light green polka dot, cut:
- 24 of Pattern C
- 12 of Pattern E

From light green print, cut:
- 4—2×26" inner border strips

From green stripe, cut:
- 4—4×33" outer border strips

Assemble Quilt Center

1. Referring to Assemble Blocks, *page 51*, Step 1, make the following AB units: 16 green-and-yellow AB units using green print A pieces and yellow print B pieces; 16 gold-and-white AB units using gold polka dot A pieces and solid white B pieces; and four white-and-green AB units using solid white A pieces and green print B pieces.

2. Referring to Assemble Blocks, Step 4, *page 52,* use light green polka dot C pieces, green-and-yellow AB units, and gold-and-white AB units to make eight green-and-yellow ABC units and eight gold-and-white ABC units **(Diagram 21)**.

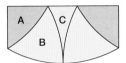

Diagram 21

3. Referring to Assemble Blocks, Step 6, use light green polka dot E pieces and white-and-green AB units to make two white-and-green ABE units **(Diagram 22)**.

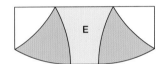

Diagram 22

4. Referring to Assemble Blocks, steps 7 and 8, use light green polka dot C pieces and green-and-yellow ABC units to make four of block 1 **(Diagram 23)**.

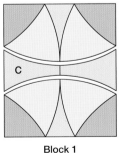

Block 1
Diagram 23

5. Referring to Assemble Blocks, steps 9 and 10, use light green polka dot E pieces and gold-and-white ABC units to make four of block 2 **(Diagram 24)**.

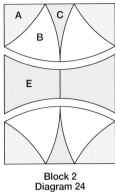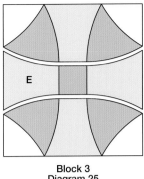

Block 2
Diagram 24

Block 3
Diagram 25

6. Referring to Assemble Blocks, steps 11 and 12, use green print 2" square, light green polka dot E pieces, and white-and-green ABE units to make one of block 3 **(Diagram 25)**.

7. Referring to photo *opposite*, lay out blocks in three rows. Sew together blocks in each row. Press seams toward block 2. Join rows to make quilt center. Press seams in one direction. The quilt center should be 20" square including seam allowances.

Add Borders

1. Aligning midpoints, join an inner border strip and an outer border strip to make a border unit. Press seam toward outer border. Repeat to make four border units total.

2. Aligning midpoints, sew border units to opposite edges of quilt center, beginning and ending seams ¼" from quilt center corners. Repeat to add remaining border units to remaining edges, mitering the corners, to complete quilt top. (For details, see Mitered Border Corners, *page 157*.) Press all seams toward border units.

Finish Quilt

1. Layer quilt top, batting, and backing; baste. (For details, see Complete the Quilt, *page 159*.)

2. Quilt as desired. Blocks on the featured quilt are outline-quilted ¼" inside each shape. The borders are stitched with horizontal lines, using the stripes as a guide.

3. Bind with green print binding strips. (For details, see Complete the Quilt.)

ON THE
Dot

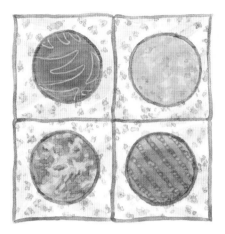

Jazz up a room with this easy-to-appliqué dotted quilt

by designer Teri Christopherson.

Materials

4½ yards gold floral (appliqué foundations)

3 yards total assorted prints in rust, green, plum, teal, pumpkin, gold, and gray (circle appliqués, border)

1¾ yards green print (border)

¾ yard rust print (binding)

5¾ yards backing fabric

79×103" batting

Lightweight fusible web

Finished quilt: 72½×96½"
Finished block: 8" square
For additional quilt sizes, see Optional Sizes chart on Pattern Sheet 2.

Quantities are for 44/45"-wide, 100% cotton fabrics. Measurements include ¼" seam allowances. Sew with right sides together unless otherwise stated.

Designer Notes

Teri Christopherson of Black Mountain Quilts first selected the rich, vibrant colors for her quilt's circle appliqués and pieced border, then found the background print.

   "I searched for an appliqué foundation fabric that would showcase these jewel-tone prints," Teri says. "This gold floral, which contains hints of the colors in the assorted prints, sets off the appliqué and border fabrics beautifully."

Cut Fabrics

Cut pieces in the following order. The Circle Pattern is on *Pattern Sheet 1*. To use fusible web for appliquéing, complete the following steps.

1. Lay fusible web, paper side up, over Circle Pattern. Use a pencil to trace pattern 70 times, leaving ½" between tracings. Cut out each fusible-web circle roughly ¼" outside traced lines. To reduce bulk, cut out fusible-web circle centers, leaving ¼" inside traced lines.

2. Following manufacturer's instructions, press fusible-web rings onto wrong sides of assorted prints; let cool. Cut out fabric circles on drawn lines. Peel off paper backings.

From gold floral, cut:
• 70—8½" squares
From assorted prints, cut:
• 52—2½×8½" rectangles
• 70 of Circle Pattern
From green print, cut:
• 50—4½×8½" rectangles
From rust print, cut:
• 9—2½×42" binding strips

continued

Appliqué Blocks

1. Referring to **Appliqué Placement Diagram**, center a print circle on a gold floral 8½" square; fuse in place.

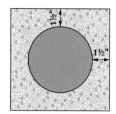

Appliqué Placement Diagram

2. Using thread that matches appliqué fabric, machine-blanket-stitch around edge of circle to make an appliquéd block.

3. Repeat steps 1 and 2 to make 70 appliquéd blocks total.

Assemble Quilt Center

1. Referring to photo *opposite* and **Quilt Assembly Diagram**, lay out appliquéd blocks in 10 rows.

2. Sew together blocks in each row. Press seams in one direction, alternating direction with each row.

3. Join rows to make quilt center. Press seams in one direction. The quilt center should be 56½×80½" including seam allowances.

Assemble and Add Border

1. Referring to **Quilt Assembly Diagram** and aligning long edges, lay out 14 assorted print 2½×8½" rectangles and 13 green print 4½×8½" rectangles, alternating assorted prints with green print; sew together to make a long border strip. Press seams toward green print. The long border strip should be 8½×80½" including seam allowances. Repeat to make a second long border strip.

2. Sew long border strips to long edges of quilt center. Press seams toward border.

3. Again aligning long edges, lay out 12 assorted print 2½×8½" rectangles and 12 green print 4½×8½" rectangles, alternating as before; sew together to make a short border strip. Press seams toward green print. The short border strip should be 8½×72½" including seam allowances. Repeat to make a second short border strip.

4. Referring to **Quilt Assembly Diagram**, sew short border strips to short edges of quilt center to complete quilt top. Press seams toward border.

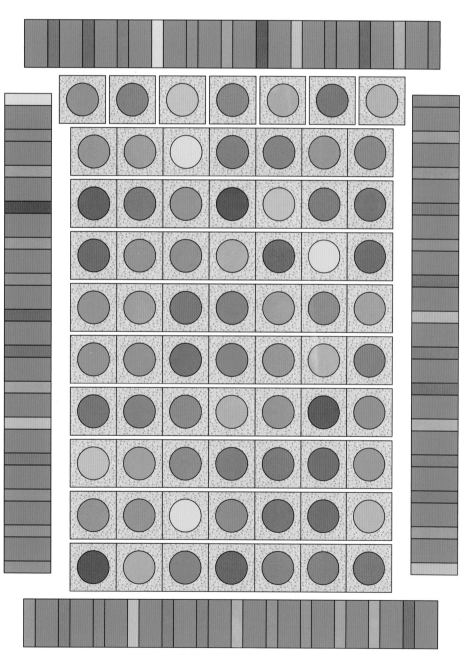

Quilt Assembly Diagram

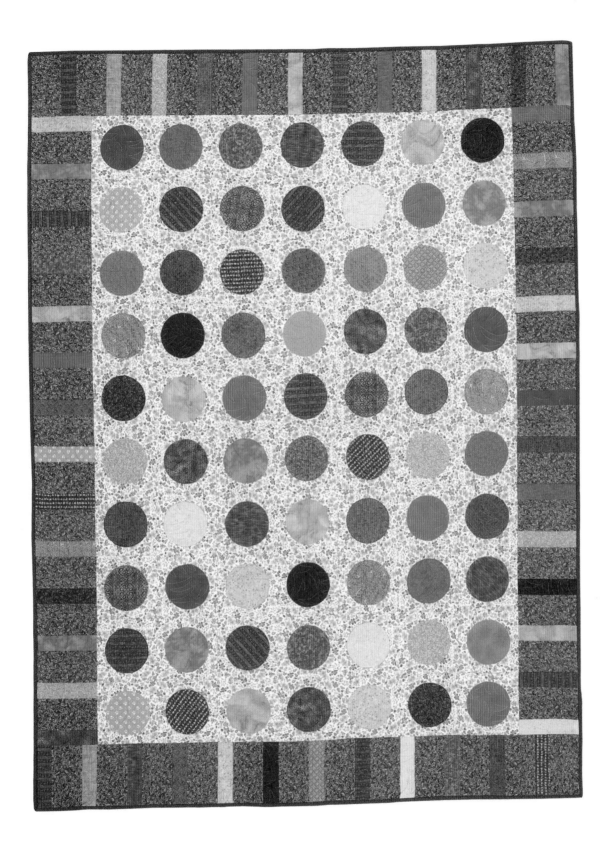

Finish Quilt

1. Layer quilt top, batting, and backing; baste. (For details, see Complete the Quilt, *page 159.*)

2. Quilt as desired. Machine-quilter Vicki Stratton quilted a palm-frond pattern over the quilt top.

3. Bind with rust print 2½×42" binding strips. (For details, see Complete the Quilt.)

SUMMER TABLECLOTH

Simple and sweet, a tablecloth is the perfect way to show off your favorite fabric.

Materials

1⅛ yards navy blue print (border)

⅓ yard total assorted gold prints (border)

¼ yard total assorted red prints (border)

¾ yard red plaid (border, binding)

1½ yards red floral (quilt center)

3⅛ yards backing fabric

Finished tablecloth: 48½×64½"

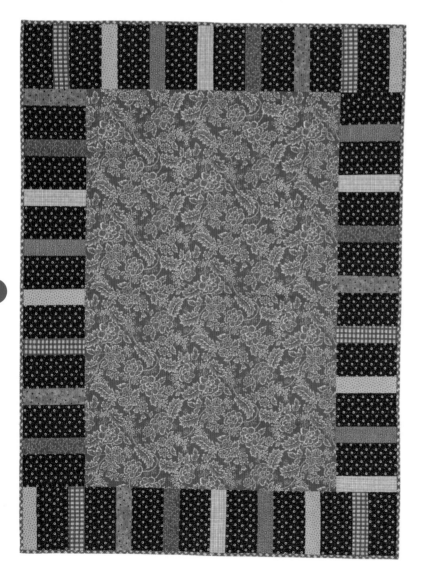

Cut Fabrics

Cut pieces in the following order.

From navy blue print, cut:
* 32—4½×8½" rectangles

From assorted gold prints, cut:
* 16—2½×8½" rectangles

From assorted red prints, cut:
* 10—2½×8½" rectangles

From red plaid, cut:
* 1—26" square, cutting it into enough 2½"-wide bias strips to total 240" for binding (For details, see Cutting Bias Strips, *page 155*.)
* 6—2½×8½" rectangles

From red floral, cut:
* 1—32½×48½" rectangle

Assemble Tablecloth Top

1. Referring to Assemble and Add Border, *page 62*, Step 1, and photo at *left*, join eight navy blue print 4½×8½" rectangles, four assorted gold print 2½×8½" rectangles, and four assorted red print or plaid 2½×8½" rectangles to make a border strip. Press seams toward navy blue print. The border strip should be 8½×48½" including seam allowances. Repeat to make four border strips total.

2. Sew border strips to long edges of red floral 32½×48½" rectangle. Join remaining border strips to remaining edges to complete tablecloth top. Press all seams toward red floral.

Finish Tablecloth

1. Layer tablecloth top and backing with wrong sides together; baste. (For details, see Complete the Quilt, *page 159*.)

2. Quilt as desired. This tablecloth was stitched in the ditch between the border and quilt center.

3. Bind with red plaid bias binding strips. (For details, see Complete the Quilt.)

BLACK-AND-WHITE THROW

A splash of yellow highlights a vibrant mix of black-and-white prints.

Materials

1½ yards total assorted white-and-black prints (blocks)

½ yard total assorted yellow prints (blocks)

2⅜ yards total assorted black-and-white prints (blocks)

¼ yard yellow-and-black print (blocks)

½ yard black tone-on-tone (binding)

3½ yards backing fabric

63" square batting

Lightweight fusible web

Finished quilt: 56½" square

Cut Fabrics

Cut pieces in the following order. This project uses *On the Dot* Circle Pattern on *Pattern Sheet 1.* To use fusible web for appliquéing, complete the following steps.

1. Lay fusible web, paper side up, over Circle Pattern. Use a pencil to trace pattern 24 times, leaving ½" between tracings. Cut out each fusible-web circle roughly ¼" outside traced lines.

2. Following manufacturer's instructions, press each fusible-web circle onto wrong side of designated fabric; let cool. Cut out fabric circles on drawn lines. Peel off paper backings.

From assorted white-and-black prints, cut:
• 12 of Circle Pattern
• 40—2½×8½" rectangles (20 pairs of matching pieces)
From assorted yellow prints, cut:
• 12 of Circle Pattern
From assorted black-and-white prints, cut:
• 24—8½" squares
• 25—4½×8½" rectangles
From yellow-and-black print, cut:
• 10—2½×8½" rectangles
From black tone-on-tone, cut:
• 6—2½×42" binding strips

Assemble Blocks

1. Referring to Appliqué Blocks, *page 62,* steps 1 and 2, use white-and-black and yellow print circles and black-and-white print 8½" squares to make 24 appliquéd blocks.

2. Sew together one black-and-white print 4½×8½" rectangle and two matching white-and-black or yellow-and-black print 2½×8½" rectangles to make a pieced block (**Block Assembly Diagram**). Press seams toward black-and-white print. The block should be 8½" square including seam allowances. Repeat to make 25 pieced blocks total.

Block Assembly Diagram

Assemble Quilt Top

1. Referring to photo *below,* lay out appliquéd blocks and pieced blocks in seven horizontal rows, alternating yellow and white-and-black appliquéd blocks and rotating the pieced blocks as shown.

2. Sew together blocks in each row. Press seams toward appliquéd blocks. Join rows to make quilt top. Press seams in one direction.

Finish Quilt

1. Layer quilt top, batting, and backing; baste. (For details, see Complete the Quilt, *page 159.*)

2. Quilt as desired. This quilt was stitched with an allover feather design using yellow thread.

3. Bind with black tone-on-tone binding strips. (For details, see Complete the Quilt.)

BOLD AND BEAUTIFUL

Some quilts stop you in your tracks with their striking

colors. The quiltmaker's choice of fabric plays a huge

role in the attitude of the finished quilts. Whether it

is bright prints or bold solids, one thing is for sure—

these quilts make a statement. Stretch your color

palette by experimenting with hues and intensities

that captivate you the moment they catch your eye.

HUNTER'S *Star*

Designer Jackie Robinson's rotary-cut wonder provides the magic of eight-pointed stars without the effort of sewing diamond shapes or setting in seams.

Materials

4⅓ yards blue-green batik (blocks, border, binding)

3½ yards light blue batik (blocks)

3⅞ yards backing fabric

69×81" batting

Acrylic ruler with 45° marking

Finished quilt: 63×75"
Finished block: 6" square
For additional quilt sizes, see Optional Sizes chart on Pattern Sheet 2.

Quantities are for 44/45"-wide, 100% cotton fabrics. Measurements include ¼" seam allowances. Sew with right sides together unless otherwise stated.

Cut Fabrics

Cut pieces in the following order.

From blue-green batik, cut:
- 7—2½×42" binding strips
- 7—1¾×42" strips for border
- 60—5⅛" squares, cutting each in half diagonally for 120 triangles total
- 120—1¾×5½" rectangles
- 240—1¾×4" rectangles

From light blue batik, cut:
- 60—5⅛" squares, cutting each in half diagonally for 120 triangles total
- 120—1¾×5½" rectangles
- 240—1¾×4" rectangles

Assemble Blocks

1. With wrong sides together, pair two blue-green batik 1¾×4" rectangles. Align the ruler's 45° line at the corner on stacked pair's long edge. Cut off corner to make a mirror-image pair (**Diagram 1**).

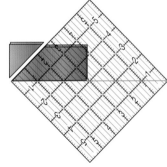

Diagram 1

2. Repeat Step 1 with all remaining blue-green and light blue batik 1¾×4" rectangles to make 120 blue-green mirror-image pairs total and 120 light blue mirror-image pairs total.

3. Use a pencil to mark a 45° line on wrong side of each mirror-image piece (**Diagram 2**; cut edge and drawn line are parallel).

Diagram 2

4. Align and sew a marked blue-green mirror-image pair to each end of a light blue batik 1¾×5½" rectangle (**Diagram 3** on *page 72*; note direction of drawn lines). Trim excess, leaving a ¼" seam allowance, to make a blue-green diamond

continued

"Select two fabrics that have a strong contrast between light and dark for the best results."

—quilt designer Jackie Robinson

strip. Press seams toward blue-green pieces. Repeat to make 120 blue-green diamond strips total.

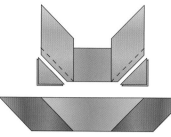

Diagram 3

5. Repeat Step 4 using marked light blue mirror-image pairs and blue-green batik $1\frac{3}{4}\times5\frac{1}{2}$" rectangles to make 120 light blue diamond strips total (**Diagram 4**). Press seams toward blue-green center.

Diagram 4

6. Sew together a blue-green diamond strip and a light blue batik triangle to make a light blue half block (**Diagram 5**). Press seam toward blue-green diamond strip. Repeat to make 120 light blue half blocks total.

Diagram 5

7. Sew together a light blue diamond strip and a blue-green batik triangle to make a blue-green half block (**Diagram 6**). Press seam toward blue-green triangle. Repeat to make 120 blue-green half blocks total.

Diagram 6

8. Sew together a light blue half block and a blue-green half block to make a Hunter's Star block (**Diagram 7**). Press seam toward blue-green half block. The block should be 6½" square including seam allowances; center and trim if necessary. Repeat to make 120 Hunter's Star blocks total.

Diagram 7

Assemble Quilt Center
1. Lay out Hunter's Star blocks in 12 horizontal rows (**Quilt Assembly Diagram**).

2. Sew together blocks in each row. Press seams in one direction, alternating direction with each row. Join rows to make quilt center. The quilt center should be 60½×72½" including seam allowances.

Add Border
1. Cut and piece blue-green batik 1¾×42" strips to make:
- 2—1¾×72½" border strips
- 2—1¾×63" border strips

2. Sew long border strips to long edges of quilt center. Sew short border strips to remaining edges to complete quilt top. Press all seams toward border.

Finish Quilt
1. Layer quilt top, batting, and backing; baste. (For details, see Complete the Quilt, *page 159.*)

2. Quilt as desired. Designer Jackie Robinson machine-quilted a diamond pattern in the center of each block. She outline-quilted each eight-pointed star where four blocks intersect, and she stitched a feathered wreath motif in the hourglass areas where blocks meet (**Quilting Diagram**).

3. Bind with blue-green batik binding strips. (For details, see Complete the Quilt.)

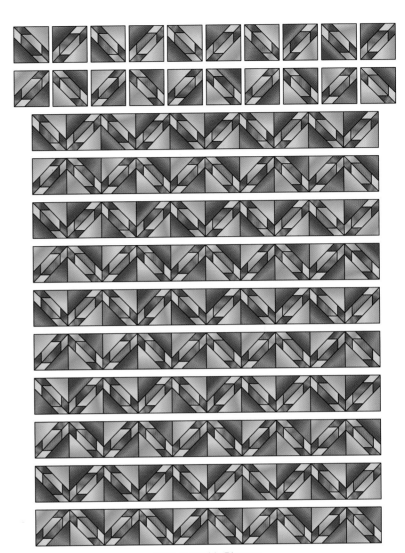

Quilt Assembly Diagram

Quilting Diagram

continued

Woodland Stars

Quilt tester Laura Boehnke used botanical prints and tone-on-tone fabrics to create her wall-hanging version of *Hunter's Star.*

"I tried to make the stars where the blocks join pop out more by having less contrast in my background fabrics," Laura says. "I think the result in the finished quilt is a muted, layered effect.

"To make sure my star colors would match up when I joined blocks, I first drew my design on graph paper with colored pencils," she says. "Then I referred to that drawing as I cut my fabrics and sewed the blocks.

"Though I used some prints as opposed to all tone-on-tone fabrics, I kept to small- and medium-scale prints that wouldn't visually interrupt the design."

MIDNIGHT STARS THROW

Dark stars pop off a light background amid a red print grid.

A scrappy mix of cream prints adds interest to the pieced background.

Materials

1½ yards total assorted black prints (blocks)

1¼ yards total assorted red prints (blocks)

1⅜ yards total assorted tan prints (blocks)

⅝ yard red tone-on-tone (inner border)

2 yards black floral (outer border, binding)

3¾ yards backing fabric

67" square batting

Finished quilt: 60½" square

Cut Fabrics

Cut pieces in the following order. Cut outer border and binding strips lengthwise (parallel to the selvages).

From assorted black prints, cut:
• 256—1¾×4" rectangles (128 pairs of matching rectangles)

From assorted red prints, cut:
• 128—1¾×5½" rectangles

From assorted tan prints, cut:
• 64—5⅛" squares, cutting each in half diagonally for 128 triangles total

From red tone-on-tone, cut:
• 7—2½×42" strips for inner border

From black floral, cut:
• 4—4½×69½" outer border strips
• 4—2½×68" binding strips

Assemble Blocks

1. Referring to Assemble Blocks, *page 71*, Step 1, use assorted black print 1¾×4" rectangles to make 128 mirror-image pairs total.

2. Referring to Assemble Blocks, steps 3 and 4, use mirror-image pairs and assorted red print rectangles to make 128 diamond strips total.

3. Referring to Assemble Blocks, Step 6, use diamond strips and assorted tan print triangles to make 128 half blocks.

4. Referring to Assemble Blocks, Step 8, join half blocks to make 64 Hunter's Star blocks total.

Assemble Quilt Center

Referring to photo on *page 76*, lay out blocks in eight rows. Sew together blocks in each row. Press seams in one direction, alternating direction with each row. Join rows to make quilt center. Press seams in one direction. The quilt center should be 48½" square including seam allowances.

continued

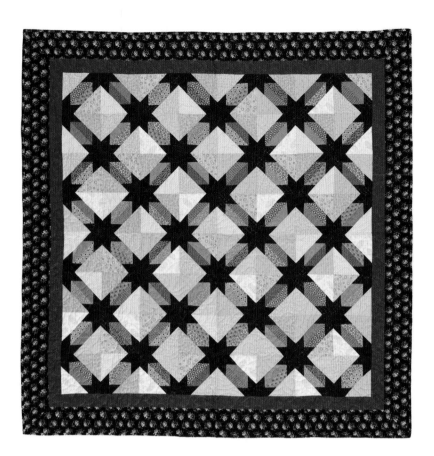

Add Borders

1. Cut and piece red tone-on-tone 2½×42" strips to make:

- 4—2½×69½" inner border strips

2. Aligning long edges, join an inner border strip and a black floral outer border strip to make a border unit. Press seam toward black floral. Repeat to make four border units total.

3. With midpoints aligned, sew border units to opposite edges of quilt center, beginning and ending seams ¼" from corners. Add remaining border units, mitering corners, to complete quilt top. (For details, see Mitered Border Corners, *page 157.*) Press all seams toward border units.

Finish Quilt

1. Layer quilt top, batting, and backing; baste. (For details, see Complete the Quilt, *page 159.*)

2. Quilt as desired. The featured quilt is stitched with an allover floral scrollwork design.

3. Bind with black floral binding strips. (For details, see Complete the Quilt.)

SERENE STARS WALL HANGING

A gentle blend of soft colors and a monochromatic background

lends a calming influence to small-space decor.

Materials

⅛ yard *each* tan print and tan tone-on-tone (blocks)

⅛ yard blue print (blocks)

½ yard blue tone-on-tone (blocks, binding)

4—¼-yard pieces assorted cream prints (blocks)

¾ yard backing fabric

31×25" batting

Finished quilt: 24½×18½"

Cut Fabrics

Cut pieces in the following order.

From tan print, cut:
- 11—1¾×4" rectangles

From tan tone-on-tone, cut:
- 11—1¾×4" rectangles

From blue print, cut:
- 13—1¾×4" rectangles

From blue tone-on-tone, cut:
- 3—2½×42" binding strips
- 13—1¾×4" rectangles

From *each* cream print, cut:
- 3—5⅛" squares, cutting each in half diagonally for 6 triangles total
- 6—1¾×5½" rectangles

Assemble Blocks

1. Refer to Assemble Blocks, *page 71*, Step 1, to make mirror-image pairs in the following fabrics:
- 6 tan print/tan tone-on-tone pairs
- 5 tan print/blue tone-on-tone pairs
- 5 blue print/tan tone-on-tone pairs
- 8 blue print/blue tone-on-tone pairs

2. Referring to Assemble Blocks, steps 3 and 4, use mirror-image pairs and assorted cream print rectangles to make 24 diamond strips total.

3. Referring to Assemble Blocks, Step 6, join a diamond strip and a cream print triangle to make a half block (triangle should match cream print used in diamond strip). Repeat with remaining diamond strips to make 24 half blocks total.

4. Referring to photo *above* for color placement and Assemble Blocks, Step 8, join half blocks to make 12 Hunter's Star blocks total.

Assemble Quilt Top

Referring to photo *above*, lay out blocks in three horizontal rows. Sew together blocks in each row. Press seams in one direction, alternating direction with each row. Join rows to make quilt top; press seams in one direction.

Finish Quilt

1. Layer quilt top, batting, and backing; baste. (For details, see Complete the Quilt, *page 159*.)

2. Quilt as desired. The featured quilt is outline-quilted ¼" inside each cream print piece and inside each eight-pointed star where four blocks intersect.

3. Bind with blue tone-on-tone binding strips. (For details, see Complete the Quilt.)

KID IN A
Candy Store

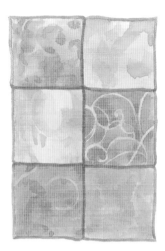

Choosing an array of fabrics to create this simple throw

was as exciting for FunQuilts designers Bill Kerr and Weeks Ringle

as being a kid in a candy shop.

Materials
Refer to Select Fabrics, *right,* for additional
    information.

⅝ yard total assorted light green prints (blocks)

⅝ yard total assorted green prints (blocks)

¾ yard total assorted aqua prints (blocks)

¾ yard total assorted yellow prints (blocks)

⅔ yard total assorted orange prints (blocks)

⅔ yard total assorted pink prints (blocks)

¾ yard total assorted purple prints (blocks)

2½ yards white print (sashing, binding)

3¼ yards backing fabric

57×78" batting

Finished quilt: 50½×71½"
Finished block: 4×6"
*For additional quilt sizes, see Optional Sizes chart
on Pattern Sheet 1.*

Quantities are for 44/45"-wide, 100% cotton fabrics.
Measurements include ¼" seam allowances. Sew
with right sides together unless otherwise stated.

Select Fabrics
Six 2½" squares of six different fabrics in a single
color compose each block of this quilt.

When selecting fabrics, look for tone-on-tone
prints. Avoid fabrics with directional prints or
large-scale patterns. The goal is to create blocks
that look unified.

Select at least six fabrics each of these seven
colors: light green, medium green, aqua, yellow,
orange, pink, and purple. Designers Bill Kerr and
Weeks Ringle used a collection of watercolor
prints as the foundation of their palette. They
supplemented those fabrics with others from their
stash to create a vibrant rainbow of color.

Bill and Weeks suggest pressing seams open
when constructing this quilt. For additional insight
into their pressing methods, see Bill and Weeks's
tips in "It Seams Different" on *page 82.*

Cut Fabrics
Cut pieces in the following order. Cut sashing strips
lengthwise (parallel to the selvages).

From assorted light green prints, cut:
• 72—2½" squares
From assorted green prints, cut:
• 72—2½" squares

continued

From assorted aqua prints, cut:
- 108—2½" squares

From assorted yellow prints, cut:
- 108—2½" squares

From assorted orange prints, cut:
- 96—2½" squares

From assorted pink prints, cut:
- 96—2½" squares

From assorted purple prints, cut:
- 108—2½" squares

From white print, cut:
- 11—1½×56½" sashing strips
- 7—2½×42" binding strips
- 120—1½×6½" sashing rectangles

Assemble Blocks

1. Sew together two different light green print 2½" squares to make a light green pair (**Diagram 1**).

Press seam in one direction. The light green pair should be 4½×2½" including seam allowances. Sew together remaining assorted light green print 2½" squares in the same manner to make 36 light green pairs total.

Diagram 1   Diagram 2

2. Referring to **Diagram 2**, lay out three light green pairs. Join pairs to make a light green block. Press seams in one direction. The block should be 4½×6½" including seam allowances. Repeat with remaining light green pairs to make 12 light green blocks total.

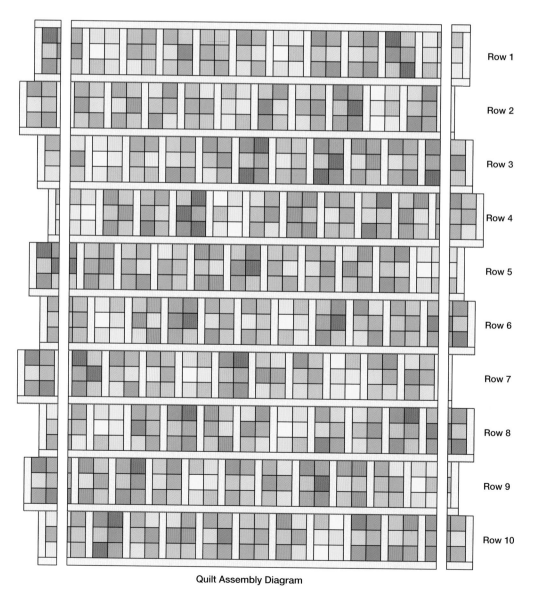

Row 1

Row 2

Row 3

Row 4

Row 5

Row 6

Row 7

Row 8

Row 9

Row 10

Quilt Assembly Diagram

3. Using remaining assorted print 2½" squares, repeat steps 1 and 2 to make an additional 98 blocks: 12 green blocks, 18 aqua blocks, 18 yellow blocks, 16 orange blocks, 16 pink blocks, and 18 purple blocks. (You will have 110 blocks total.)

Assemble Quilt Top

The following instructions use an improvisational piecing method to give the quilt a random look. Each row is shifted slightly to the left or right before joining it to the others. After rows are joined, the quilt top is trimmed to its finished size.

1. Referring to **Quilt Assembly Diagram** for color placement, lay out blocks and white print sashing rectangles in 10 horizontal rows.

2. Sew together pieces in each row. Press seams toward sashing. Each row should be 6½×56½" including seam allowances.

3. Join a white print sashing strip to bottom of each row; press seams in one direction. Sew remaining white print sashing strip to top of first row.

4. Referring to **Quilt Assembly Diagram**, lay out rows on the floor or on a design wall; slightly shift rows to left or right (between 1½" and 2½") until you are pleased with the layout. Sew rows together to complete quilt top; press seams in one direction.

5. Trim side edges so that quilt top measures 50½×71½" including seam allowances.

Finish Quilt

1. Layer quilt top, batting, and backing; baste. (For details, see Complete the Quilt, *page 159.*)

2. Quilt as desired. Bill and Weeks machine-quilted the sashing with dense stippling and the blocks with small circles.

3. Bind with white print binding strips. (For details, see Complete the Quilt.)

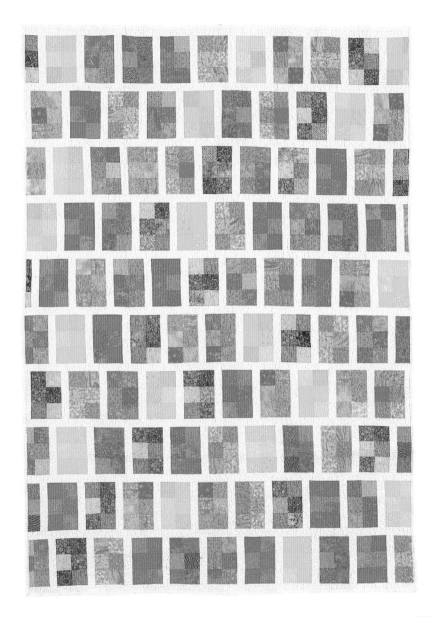

"This quilt is a great way to use up fabrics you've accumulated, as well as a great reason to head to your local quilt shop to get new ones."

—quilt designer Weeks Ringle

continued

It Seams Different

Designers Bill Kerr and Weeks Ringle have a different take on pressing seam allowances than do most quilters—they usually press them open.

"We advocate ironing all seam allowances open if you will be machine-piecing and machine-quilting," Bill says. "Seam allowances that have been ironed open lie flat, giving the quilt a crisp, graphic quality.

"Some quilters fear that ironing seam allowances open puts too much stress on the seams, but we find that machine-quilting provides plenty of reinforcement of the machine-piecing. The cotton of your quilt will most likely wear out long before the seams pull out."

"Ironing seam allowances open also makes it easier to align block units," Weeks says, "because you can slide pins between the seams to line one unit up with another.

"If you are hand-piecing, your stitch length is likely to be longer than that of a sewing machine, so you will want to iron the seam allowances to one side to prevent fiber migration from the batting."

optional colors

Color Blocks

A contrast in lights and darks, quilt tester Laura Boehnke's version of *Kid in a Candy Store* tells a different story. Using batiks for the pieced blocks and dark blue batik sashing, she created a dramatic wall hanging.

"I wanted to apply the same color principles to my version that the original quilt had—six pieces per block with subtle shifts in color," Laura says. "Batiks come in a range of colors that enabled me to accomplish that goal.

"I could also see this pattern made in tropical bright batiks with turquoise sashing."

SQUARE-DEAL SHOWER CURTAIN

Dress up a purchased shower curtain with a band of colorful squares.

Materials

¾ yard total assorted light blue, light green, and light orange prints

Fabric shower curtain

Cut Fabrics

The border strip will fit a shower curtain up to 72" wide. If your shower curtain is wider, adjust the number of blocks as needed to fit.

From assorted light blue, light green, and light orange prints, cut:
- 108—2½" squares

Assemble and Add Border

1. Referring to Assemble Blocks, *page 80*, steps 1 and 2, use assorted light blue, light green, and light orange print squares to make 18 blocks total.

2. Join blocks along long edges to make a border strip. Press seams in one direction. The border strip should be 6½×72½" including seam allowances.

3. Referring to photo *above,* center border strip on curtain 1½" from bottom hem. If necessary, trim ends of border strip ¼" beyond side edges of curtain. Press under a ¼" seam allowance on all edges of border strip. Reposition border on curtain and generously pin in place. Topstitch all edges of border to curtain.

PATCHWORK SQUARES QUILT

Love scrap quilts? This one is perfect for using up your fabric bits and pieces.

Kid in a Candy Store

Materials

4 yards total assorted green, red, yellow, and blue prints, stripes, and polka dots (blocks)

4½ yards mottled dark blue (sashing, border, binding)

¼ yard red print (piping)

5⅔ yards backing fabric

73×102" batting

Finished quilt: 66½×95½"

Cut Fabrics

Cut pieces in the following order. Cut sashing, border, and binding strips lengthwise (parallel to the selvages).

From assorted green, red, yellow, and blue prints, stripes, and polka dots, cut:
• 792—2½" squares

From mottled dark blue, cut:
• 2—6½×83½" border strips
• 2—6½×66½" border strips
• 11—1½×54½" sashing strips
• 7—2½×50" binding strips
• 120—1½×6½" sashing rectangles

From red print, cut:
• 8—¾×42" strips for piping

Assemble Blocks

Referring to Assemble Blocks, *page 80,* steps 1 and 2, use assorted print, stripe, and polka dot squares to make 132 blocks total.

Assemble Quilt Top

1. Referring to photo at *right,* lay out blocks, sashing rectangles, and sashing strips in 23 horizontal rows. Join pieces in each row; press seams toward sashing rectangles. Join rows and sashing strips to complete quilt center. Press seams toward sashing strips. The quilt center should be 54½×83½" including seam allowances.

2. Sew long border strips to long edges of quilt center. Add short border strips to remaining edges to complete quilt top. Press all seams toward border.

Finish Quilt

1. Layer quilt top, batting, and backing; baste. (For details, see Complete the Quilt, *page 159.*)

2. Quilt as desired. The featured quilt is stitched with an allover vine and leaf design using variegated thread. A narrow pebble design is quilted in the border next to each sashing strip.

3. Cut and piece red print ¾×42" strips to make:
• 2—¾×95½" piping strips
• 2—¾×66½" piping strips

4. With wrong side inside, fold each piping strip in half lengthwise; press. Aligning raw edges, baste short piping strips to short edges of quilt top using a scant ¼" seam allowance. Baste long piping strips to remaining edges.

5. Bind with mottled dark blue binding strips. (For details, see Complete the Quilt.) (About ⅛" of the red piping will show between quilt top and binding edge after binding is turned to the back.)

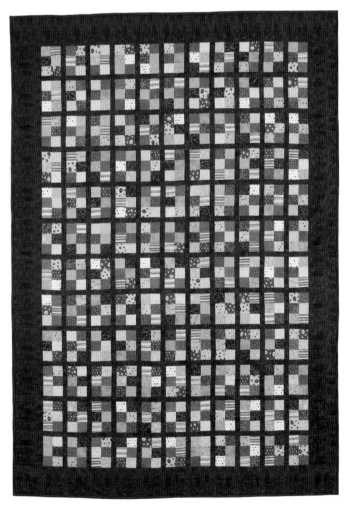

TILTED
Mountains

The splendor and majesty of the nearby Rocky Mountains gave
Nancy Smith and Lynda Milligan of Possibilities the idea of creating
slightly askew strip-pieced blocks using a fun, free-form technique.

Materials
9—½-yard pieces assorted purple prints (blocks)

2⅜ yards total assorted purple prints and green prints (blocks)

⅜ yard red-violet print (inner border)

7—⅓-yard pieces assorted bright green prints (middle border)

2¼ yards purple batik (outer border, binding)

5 yards backing fabric

72×90" batting

Finished quilt: 65½×83½"
Finished block: 9" square
For additional quilt sizes, see Optional Sizes chart on Pattern Sheet 2.

Quantities are for 44/45"-wide, 100% cotton fabrics. Measurements include ¼" seam allowances. Sew with right sides together unless otherwise stated.

Cut Fabrics
Cut pieces in the following order.

From assorted purple prints, cut:
- 108—2×21" strips

From assorted purple prints and green prints, cut:
- 70 sets of 2—3⅞" squares, cutting each in half diagonally for 280 triangles total (70 sets of 4 matching triangles)
- 35—3½" squares

From red-violet print, cut:
- 6—1½×42" strips for inner border

From *each* assorted bright green print, cut:
- 8—2×21" strips

From purple batik, cut:
- 8—6½×42" strips for outer border
- 8—2½×42" binding strips

Assemble Pieced Squares
1. Sew together two assorted purple print 2×21" strips, slightly offsetting strips. Trim seam allowance to ¼"; press seam in one direction. Continue adding purple print 2×21" strips, alternating angle from right side to left side to keep emerging rectangle from curving, until you have a pieced rectangle approximately 21×54". Press and trim seams to ¼" after each strip is added. Repeat with remaining purple print 2×21" strips to make a second pieced rectangle.

continued

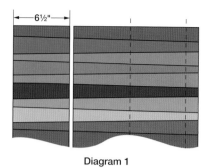

Diagram 1

2. Cut each pieced rectangle into 6½"-wide strips (**Diagram 1**). Cut each 6½"-wide strip into 6½" squares for 35 pieced squares total (**Diagram 2**).

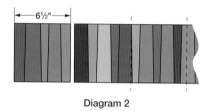

Diagram 2

Assemble Triangle-Squares

1. Select two sets of purple print triangles.

2. Sew together one purple print triangle from each set to make a triangle-square (**Diagram 3**). Press seam in one direction. The triangle-square should be 3½" square including seam allowances. Repeat to make a set of four matching triangle-squares.

Diagram 3

3. Repeat steps 1 and 2 with remaining sets of purple and green print triangles to make 35 sets total of four matching triangle-squares. (Some triangle-square sets will include green print and purple print triangles.)

Assemble Blocks

1. Lay out one pieced square, one set of four matching triangle-squares, and one purple or green print 3½" square (**Diagram 4**).

Diagram 4

2. Sew together pieces in sections. Press seams in one direction. Join sections to make a block. Press seam in one direction. The block should be 9½" square including seam allowances.

3. Repeat steps 1 and 2 to make 35 blocks total. For 18 of the 35 blocks, orient pieced square with strips running horizontally as shown in **Diagram 4**. For remaining 17 blocks, turn pieced square so strips run vertically.

Assemble Quilt Center

1. Lay out blocks in seven horizontal rows (**Quilt Assembly Diagram**).

2. Sew together blocks in each row. Press seams in one direction, alternating direction with each row. Join rows to make quilt center. Press seams in one direction. The quilt center should be 45½×63½" including seam allowances.

Assemble and Add Borders

1. Cut and piece red-violet print 1½×42" strips to make:
- 2—1½×63½" inner border strips
- 2—1½×47½" inner border strips

2. Sew long inner border strips to long edges of quilt center. Sew short inner border strips to remaining edges. Press all seams toward inner border.

3. Sew together two assorted bright green print 2×21" strips, slightly offsetting strips. Trim seam allowance to ¼"; press seam in one direction. Continue adding bright green print 2×21" strips, alternating angle from right side to left side to keep emerging rectangle from curving, until you have a pieced rectangle approximately 21×28". Press and trim seams to ¼" after each strip is added. Repeat with remaining bright green print 2×21" strips to make a second pieced rectangle.

4. Cut each pieced rectangle into 3½"-wide strips to make 10—3½×28" border units total (**Diagram 5**).

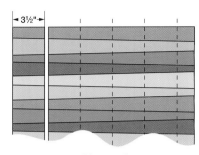

◄ 3½" ►

Diagram 5

5. Cut and piece border units to make:
- 2—3½×65½" middle border strips
- 2—3½×53½" middle border strips

6. Sew long middle border strips to long edges of quilt center. Join short middle border strips to remaining edges. Press all seams toward inner border.

7. Cut and piece purple batik 6½×42" strips to make:
- 2—6½×71½" outer border strips
- 2—6½×65½" outer border strips

8. Sew long outer border strips to long edges of quilt center. Add short outer border strips to remaining edges to complete quilt top. Press all seams toward outer border.

Finish Quilt

1. Layer quilt top, batting, and backing; baste. (For details, see Complete the Quilt, *page 159*.)

2. Quilt as desired. Machine-quilter Ann Petersen quilted an allover loose feather motif and echoes in the quilt center (**Quilting Diagram**). She quilted a wavy line over every seam in the bright green middle border. In the outer border she repeated the free-motion feather design.

3. Bind with purple batik binding strips. (For details, see Complete the Quilt.)

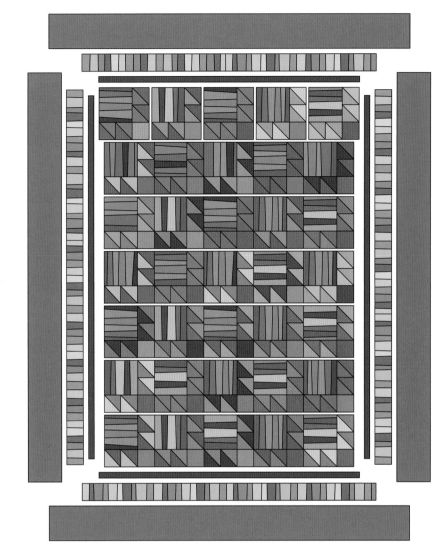

Quilt Assembly Diagram

Quilting Diagram

Tilted Mountains

continued

Adding a splash of green in the blocks not only helps tie in the pieced middle border, but also adds interest to the finished quilt.

optional colors

Getting to the Point

Because of deliberate attention to the placement of lights and darks in the triangle-squares, the points of the blocks stand out more in quilt tester Laura Boehnke's 12-block wall hanging than they do in the original quilt. Laura also rotated the blocks so the points face up.

"This quilt pattern has so many possibilities. After I'd pieced the blocks and rotated them, it took my mind in yet another direction I'd like to try," Laura says. "The blocks remind me of a summer sunrise early in the morning. I'm planning to make another version with reds, yellows, and oranges."

SCRAPPY TABLE TOPPER

Four scrappy star blocks set the stage for a stunning small quilt.

Materials

1¾ yards total assorted green, red, orange, tan, and black prints (blocks, outer border)

¼ yard mottled dark green (inner border)

⅜ yard black print (binding)

1⅛ yards backing fabric

39" square batting

Finished quilt: 32½" square
Finished block: 12" square

Cut Fabrics

Cut pieces in the following order.

From assorted green, red, orange, tan, and black prints, cut:
- 28—2×21" strips
- 32—3⅞" squares, cutting each in half diagonally for 64 triangles total
- 32—3½" squares

From mottled dark green, cut:
- 2—1½×26½" inner border strips
- 2—1½×24½" inner border strips

From black print, cut:
- 4—2½×42" binding strips

Assemble Quilt Center

1. Referring to Assemble Triangle-Squares, *page 88,* Step 2, use assorted print triangles to make 32 triangle-squares total.

2. Referring to **Diagram 6**, lay out eight triangle-squares and eight assorted print 3½" squares in four rows; note direction of seams in triangle-squares. Sew together pieces in each row. Press seams in one direction, alternating direction with each row. Join rows to make a star block; press seams in one direction. The star block should be 12½" square including seam allowances. Repeat to make four star blocks total.

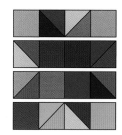

Diagram 6

continued

3. Referring to photo *above,* sew together star blocks in pairs. Press seams in opposite directions. Join pairs to make quilt center. Press seam in one direction. The quilt center should be 24½" square including seam allowances.

Assemble and Add Borders

1. Sew short inner border strips to opposite edges of quilt center. Sew long inner border strips to remaining edges. Press all seams toward inner border.

2. Referring to Assemble and Add Borders, *page 88,* Step 3, sew together assorted print 2×21" strips to make a 21×28" pieced rectangle.

3. Referring to Assemble and Add Borders, Step 4, cut pieced rectangle into five 3½×28" border units.

4. Cut and piece border units to make:
- 2—3½×32½" outer border strips
- 2—3½×26½" outer border strips

5. Sew short outer border strips to opposite edges of quilt center. Join long outer border strips to remaining edges to complete quilt top. Press all seams toward inner border.

Finish Quilt

1. Layer quilt top, batting, and backing; baste. (For details, see Complete the Quilt, *page 159.*)

2. Quilt as desired. The featured quilt is stitched with swirl, wave, and zigzag motifs.

3. Bind with black print binding strips. (For details, see Complete the Quilt.)

REPRODUCTION PRINT THROW

Stripes surround the stars on a throw of Civil War reproduction fabrics.

Materials

1⅜ yards total assorted red and dark pink prints (blocks)

12—¼-yard pieces assorted tan prints (blocks)

1¾ yards total assorted medium and dark prints (blocks)

¼ yard red print (sashing)

2¾ yards blue stripe (sashing, binding)

2⅛ yards burgundy stripe (border)

7⅛ yards backing fabric

85×106" batting

Finished quilt: 78½×99½"
Finished four-block unit: 18"

Cut Fabrics

Cut pieces in the following order.

From assorted red and dark pink prints, cut:
- 96—3⅞" squares, cutting each in half diagonally for 192 triangles total

From *each* tan print, cut:
- 8—3⅞" squares, cutting each in half diagonally for 16 triangles total (12 sets of 16 matching triangles)
- 4—3½" squares

From assorted medium and dark prints, cut:
- 48—6½" squares

From red print, cut:
- 20—3½" sashing squares

From blue stripe, cut:
- 31—3½×18½" sashing rectangles (cut 15 with stripes running vertically; cut 16 with stripes running horizontally)
- 9—2½×42" binding strips (cut with stripes running vertically)

From burgundy stripe, cut:
- 10—6½×42" strips for border

Assemble Block Units

1. Referring to Assemble Triangle-Squares, *page 88*, Step 2, use assorted red and dark pink print triangles and matching tan print triangles to make four triangle-squares.

2. Lay out an assorted print 6½" square, triangle-squares, and a 3½" square from the matching tan print **(Diagram 7 on *page 94*)**. Referring to Assemble Blocks, *page 88*, Step 2, join pieces to make a block.

continued

Diagram 7

3. Repeat steps 1 and 2 to make four blocks total using matching tan print pieces.

4. Sew together blocks in pairs (**Diagram 8**). Press seams in opposite directions. Join pairs to make a block unit. Press seam in one direction. The block unit should be 18½" square including seam allowances.

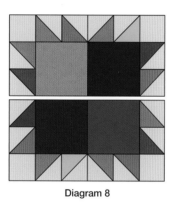

Diagram 8

5. Repeat steps 1 through 4 to make 12 block units total.

Assemble Quilt Center

1. Referring to photo on *page 93,* lay out sashing squares, sashing rectangles, and block units in nine horizontal rows. Join pieces in each row. Press seams toward sashing rectangles.

2. Join rows to make quilt center; press seams toward sashing rows. The quilt center should be 66½×87½" including seam allowances.

Add Border

1. Cut and piece burgundy stripe 6½×42" strips to make:
- 2—6½×87½" border strips
- 2—6½×78½" border strips

2. Sew long border strips to long edges of quilt center. Join short border strips to remaining edges to complete quilt top. Press all seams toward border.

Finish Quilt

1. Layer quilt top, batting, and backing; baste. (For details, see Complete the Quilt, *page 159.*)

2. Quilt as desired. The featured quilt is stitched with a feathered wreath design in the center of each block unit, overlapping half-circles in the sashing rectangles, and parallel lines in the border.

3. Bind with blue stripe binding strips. (For details, see Complete the Quilt.)

TIP: *Experiment with placement of the block units before assembling the quilt center. To evenly distribute contrast on a scrappy quilt, try squinting. Pay attention to where the lightest lights and darkest darks fall across the quilt top. Closing your eyes slightly limits the amount of light they receive and reduces your perception of color, so contrast becomes more evident.*

ROTARY
QUICK-TO-CUT

Few tools have done more to revolutionize quilting

than the rotary cutter. Say goodbye to templates,

so long to scissors, and hello to the time-saving trio

of rotary cutter, ruler, and cutting mat. The benefits?

Accurately cut pieces in a jiffy that fit together

perfectly when you sit down to sew.

Try your hand at one of these rotary-cut

wonders. You'll be under a new quilt in no time!

110

118

126

108

MAKE YOUR
Point

Designer Mabeth Oxenreider's scrappy sensation is composed of two straight-set

blocks. Careful color placement creates the illusion that they're set on point.

Materials

5¼ yards total assorted dark prints
(16-Patch blocks, Pinwheel blocks, dogtooth
border, diagonally pieced borders)

4¼ yards total assorted light prints
(16-Patch blocks, Pinwheel blocks, dogtooth
border)

¾ yard red print (binding)

5⅓ yards backing fabric

84×96" batting

Finished quilt: 78×90"
Finished blocks: 6" square

Quantities are for 44/45"-wide, 100% cotton fabrics.
Measurements include ¼" seam allowances. Sew
with right sides together unless otherwise stated.

Designer Notes

Designer Mabeth Oxenreider loves scrap quilts,
and her scrappy designs have been favorites among
quilters for years.

   "I love to take something simple, like the
16-Patch and Pinwheel blocks in this quilt, and
make them look more complicated by the way
the blocks come together," Mabeth says. "It's the
placement of the darks and lights in the Pinwheel

blocks that creates the strong diagonal lines your
eyes focus on in the finished quilt. It appears that
the entire quilt center is set on point when, in fact,
the blocks are just alternated side by side."

Cut Fabrics

Cut pieces in the following order.

From assorted dark prints, cut:
• 38—2×42" strips
• Enough 2½"-wide strips in lengths varying
  from 8" to 22" to total 400" for outer border
• Enough 1½"-wide strips in lengths varying
  from 8" to 22" to total 340" for inner and
  middle borders
• Enough 1⅛"-wide strips in lengths varying
  from 8" to 22" to total 340" for inner and
  middle borders
• 16—5½" squares, cutting each diagonally twice
  in an X for 64 triangles total (you will use 62)
• 98—3⅞" squares

From assorted light prints, cut:
• 38—2×42" strips
• 15—5½" squares, cutting each diagonally twice
  in an X for 60 triangles total (you will use 58)
• 98—3⅞" squares

From red print, cut:
• 9—2½×42" binding strips

continued

Assemble 16-Patch Blocks

1. Aligning long edges, lay out two dark print 2×42" strips and two light print 2×42" strips; sew together to make a strip set (**Diagram 1**). Press seams toward dark print strips. Repeat with remaining 2×42" strips to make 19 strip sets total. Cut strip sets into 396—2"-wide segments total. Set aside four segments for outer border.

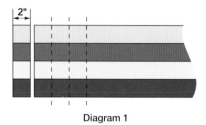

Diagram 1

2. Lay out four segments as shown in **Diagram 2**. Sew together segments to make a 16-Patch block. Press seams in one direction. The block should be 6½" square including seam allowances. Repeat to make 98—16-Patch blocks total.

Diagram 2

Assemble Pinwheel Blocks

1. Use a pencil to mark a diagonal line on wrong side of each light print 3⅞" square.

2. Layer a marked light print 3⅞" square atop each dark print 3⅞" square. Sew each pair together with two seams, stitching ¼" on each side of drawn line (**Diagram 3**).

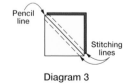

Diagram 3

To save time, chain-piece the layered squares. To chain-piece, machine-sew pairs together one after the other without lifting the presser foot or clipping threads between pairs. First sew along one side of the drawn lines, then turn the group of pairs around and sew along other side of the lines (**Diagram 4**). Clip connecting threads between pairs.

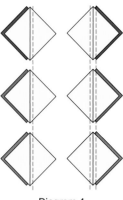

Diagram 4

3. Cut a pair apart on drawn line to make two triangle units (**Diagram 5**). Press triangle units open to make two triangle-squares (**Diagram 6**). Each triangle-square should be 3½" square including seam allowances. Repeat to make 196 triangle-squares total.

Diagram 5   Diagram 6

4. Referring to **Diagram 7** for placement, join four triangle-squares in pairs. Press seams in opposite directions. Join pairs to make a Pinwheel block A. Press seam in one direction. The block should be 6½" square including seam allowances. Repeat to make 24 total of Pinwheel block A.

5. Referring to **Diagram 8**, repeat Step 4 to make 25 total of Pinwheel block B.

Diagram 7   Diagram 8

Assemble Quilt Center

1. Referring to **Quilt Assembly Diagram**, lay out 50—16-Patch blocks and Pinwheel blocks A and B in 11 horizontal rows.

2. Sew together blocks in each row. Press seams toward Pinwheel blocks. Join rows to make quilt center. Press seams in one direction. The quilt center should be 54½×66½" including seam allowances.

Make Your Point

Quilt Assembly Diagram

Assemble and Add Inner Border

1. Using diagonal seams, sew together assorted dark print 1½"-wide strips of varying lengths to make:
- 2—1½×54½" inner border strips

2. Using diagonal seams, sew together assorted dark print 1⅛"-wide strips of varying lengths to make:
- 2—1⅛×68½" inner border strips

3. Sew short inner border strips to short edges of quilt center. Join long inner border strips to remaining edges. Press all seams toward quilt center. The quilt center should now be 55¾×68½" including seam allowances.

continued

Assemble and Add Dogtooth Border

1. Referring to **Quilt Assembly Diagram** on *page 101*, lay out 13 assorted light print triangles and 12 assorted dark print triangles in a row.

2. Layer two adjacent triangles with raw edges aligned and ends offset by ⅜" (**Diagram 9**); sew together. Press seam toward dark print. Add next triangle in row to joined triangles in same manner (**Diagram 10**). Join remaining triangles in row to make a short dogtooth border strip.

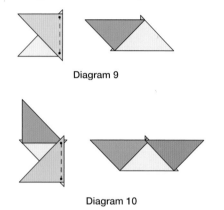

Diagram 9

Diagram 10

3. Repeat steps 1 and 2 to make a second short dogtooth border strip.

4. Fold a short dogtooth border strip in half lengthwise; use a pencil to mark center. Repeat to mark center of one short edge of quilt center. Aligning center marks, pin short dogtooth border strip to short edge of quilt center; sew together. Press seam toward inner border. Repeat with remaining short dogtooth border strip and opposite short edge of quilt center.

5. Repeat Step 2 using 16 assorted light print triangles and 15 assorted dark print triangles to make a long dogtooth border strip. Repeat to make a second long dogtooth border strip.

6. Repeat Step 4 to add long dogtooth border strips to long edges of quilt center.

7. Sew together eight remaining dark print triangles in pairs to make four border corners (**Quilt Assembly Diagram**). Press seams in one direction. Join border corners to quilt center; press seams toward corners. The quilt center should now be 60×72¾" including seam allowances.

Assemble and Add Middle Border

1. Using diagonal seams, sew together remaining assorted dark print 1⅛"-wide strips of varying lengths to make:
  - 2—1⅛×60" middle border strips

2. Using diagonal seams, sew together remaining assorted dark print 1½"-wide strips of varying lengths to make:
  - 2—1½×74" middle border strips

3. Sew short middle border strips to short edges of quilt center. Join long middle border strips to remaining edges; press all seams toward quilt center. The quilt center should now be 62×74" including seam allowances.

Assemble and Add 16-Patch Border

1. Referring to **Quilt Assembly Diagram**, lay out remaining 16-Patch blocks in four rows of 12 blocks each. Sew together blocks in each row to make four 16-Patch border strips. Press seams in one direction.

2. Add a reserved 2"-wide segment to one end of each 16-Patch border strip (**Quilt Assembly Diagram**; note color placement). Press seams in one direction.

3. Join a 16-Patch border strip to each long edge of quilt center. Press seams toward quilt center.

4. Sew remaining 16-Patch border strips to remaining edges of quilt center. Press seams toward quilt center. The quilt center should now be 74×86" including seam allowances.

Assemble and Add Outer Border

1. Using diagonal seams, sew together dark print 2½" strips of varying lengths to make:
  - 2—2½×90" outer border strips
  - 2—2½×74" outer border strips

2. Sew short outer border strips to short edges of quilt center. Join long outer border strips to remaining edges to complete quilt top. Press all seams toward quilt center.

Finish Quilt

1. Layer quilt top, batting, and backing; baste. (For details, see Complete the Quilt, *page 159*.)

2. Quilt as desired. Mabeth machine-quilted the center with an overall feather design. She used ¼" outline quilting to enhance the dogtooth border and added straight stitches in the 16-Patch border and outer border.

3. Bind with red print 2½×42" binding strips. (For details, see Complete the Quilt.)

continued

optional colors

Fields of Florals

Quilt tester Laura Boehnke used springtime florals and light prints for her 25-block wall hanging.

"The original quilt was so balanced in its use of lights and darks that your eye is drawn equally to both the Pinwheel blocks and the 16-Patch blocks," Laura says. "For my version, I tried to make the 16-Patch blocks recede by making them of only light and white prints with little contrast. To make your eye focus more on the Pinwheel blocks, I used strong, saturated colors against a single light print in the triangle-squares."

ON-POINT THROW

A new design emerges when the blocks are turned and set on point.

Materials

2 yards total assorted prints in blue, red, orange, green, and yellow (16-Patch blocks, Pinwheel blocks)

⅛ yard *each* ecru-and-blue, ecru-and-light blue, and ecru-and-red stripe (16-Patch blocks)

1 yard ecru-and-green stripe (16-Patch blocks, Pinwheel blocks)

⅝ yard blue floral (setting and corner triangles)

½ yard dark blue pin dot (16-Patch blocks, Pinwheel block, inner border)

1½ yards green floral (16-Patch blocks, Pinwheel block, outer border, binding)

3⅓ yards backing fabric

59×67" batting

Finished quilt: 52½×61"

Cut Fabrics

Cut pieces in the following order.

From assorted prints, cut:
- 14—2×42" strips
- 56—3⅞" squares (28 sets of two matching squares)

From *each* ecru-and-blue, ecru-and-light blue, and ecru-and-red stripe, cut:
- 1—2×42" strip

From ecru-and-green stripe, cut:
- 1—2×42" strip
- 60—3⅞" squares

From blue floral, cut:
- 5—9¾" squares, cutting each diagonally twice in an X for 20 setting triangles total (you will use 18)
- 2—5⅛" squares, cutting each in half diagonally for 4 corner triangles total

From dark blue pin dot, cut:
- 1—2×42" strip
- 5—1½×42" strips for inner border
- 2—3⅞" squares

continued

From green floral, cut:
- 6—4¼×42" strips for outer border
- 6—2½×42" binding strips
- 1—2×42" strip
- 2—3⅞" squares

Assemble Blocks

1. Referring to Assemble 16-Patch Blocks, *page 100*, Step 1, use the 14 assorted print, four ecru stripe, dark blue pin dot, and green floral 2×42" strips to make five strip sets (some strip sets will have one ecru stripe fabric; others will have none). Cut strip sets into 80—2"-wide segments total.

2. Referring to Assemble 16-Patch Blocks, Step 2, use segments to make 20—16-Patch blocks total.

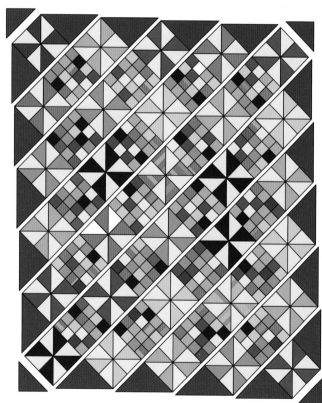

Quilt Assembly Diagram

3. Referring to Assemble Pinwheel Blocks, *page 100*, steps 1 through 3, use ecru-and-green stripe 3⅞" squares and assorted print, dark blue pin dot, and green floral 3⅞" squares to make 120 triangle-squares total (30 sets of four matching triangle-squares).

4. Referring to Assemble Pinwheel Blocks, steps 4 and 5, and using matching triangle-squares in each block, make 15 total of Pinwheel block A and 15 total of Pinwheel block B.

Assemble Quilt Top

1. Lay out 16-Patch blocks, A and B Pinwheel blocks, and blue floral setting triangles in 10 diagonal rows (**Quilt Assembly Diagram**).

2. Sew together pieces in each row; press seams in one direction, alternating direction with each row. Join rows; press seams in one direction. Add corner triangles to make quilt center. The quilt center should be 43×51½" including seam allowances.

3. Cut and piece dark blue pin dot 1½×42" strips to make:
- 2—1½×53½" inner border strips
- 2—1½×43" inner border strips

4. Sew short inner border strips to short edges of quilt center. Join long inner border strips to remaining edges. Press all seams toward inner border.

5. Cut and piece green floral 4¼×42" strips to make:
- 2—4¼×61" outer border strips
- 2—4¼×45" outer border strips

6. Sew short outer border strips to short edges of quilt center. Join long outer border strips to remaining edges to complete quilt top. Press all seams toward outer border.

Finish Quilt

1. Layer quilt top, batting, and backing; baste. (For details, see Complete the Quilt, *page 159.*)

2. Quilt as desired. This quilt was machine-quilted in an allover floral-and-leaf design.

3. Bind with green floral binding strips. (For details, see Complete the Quilt.)

PILLOWCASE TRIO

Choose prints that reflect overnight guests'
favorite things for a personalized welcome.

Materials for tan pillowcase

⅞ yard tan print (pillowcase body)

¼ yard black swirl print (sashing, dogtooth border)

12" square *each* of black-and-brown print, black dot, red check, and red print (dogtooth border)

Finished pillowcase: 20¾×31½"
(fits a standard-size bed pillow)

Cut Fabrics

Cut pieces in the following order.

From tan print, cut:
- 1—42×22¼" rectangle
- 1—42×7½" rectangle

From black swirl print, cut:
- 2—1½×42" sashing strips
- 2—5½" squares, cutting each diagonally twice in an X for 8 triangles total

From *each* of black-and-brown print and black dot, cut:
- 2—5½" squares, cutting each diagonally twice in an X for 8 triangles total

From *each* of red check and red print, cut:
- 3—5½" squares, cutting each diagonally twice in an X for 12 triangles total

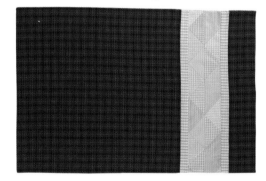

Materials for navy plaid pillowcase

⅞ yard navy plaid (pillowcase body)

⅛ yard tan stripe (sashing)

12" square *each* of tan check, solid tan, blue check, and blue stripe (dogtooth border)

Finished pillowcase: 20¾×31½"
(fits a standard-size bed pillow)

Cut Fabrics

Cut pieces in the following order.

From navy plaid, cut:
• 1—42×22¼" rectangle
• 1—42×7½" rectangle

From tan stripe, cut:
• 2—1½×42" sashing strips

From *each* of tan check, solid tan, blue check, and blue stripe, cut:
• 3—5½" squares, cutting each diagonally twice in an X for 12 triangles total

Materials for 1930s print pillowcase

⅞ yard 1930s blue print (pillowcase body)

¼ yard gold print (sashing, dogtooth border)

¼ yard red tone-on-tone (dogtooth border)

12" square mottled blue (dogtooth border)

6" square mottled green (dogtooth border)

Finished pillowcase: 20¾×31½"
(fits a standard-size bed pillow)

Cut Fabrics

Cut pieces in the following order.

From 1930s blue print, cut:
• 1—42×22¼" rectangle
• 1—42×7½" rectangle

From gold print, cut:
• 2—1½×42" sashing strips
• 3—5½" squares, cutting each diagonally twice in an X for 12 triangles total

From red tone-on-tone, cut:
• 5—5½" squares, cutting each diagonally twice in an X for 20 triangles total

From mottled blue, cut:
• 2—5½" squares, cutting each diagonally twice in an X for 8 triangles total

From mottled green, cut:
• 1—5½" square, cutting it diagonally twice in an X for 4 triangles total

Assemble Pillowcase Border

1. Referring to Assemble and Add Dogtooth Border, *page 102,* steps 1 and 2, and photo *opposite,* join 21 triangles to make a dogtooth border strip. Repeat to make a second dogtooth border strip. (You will have some triangles left over.)

2. Sew together dogtooth border strips to make a pieced band (**Diagram 11**). Press seam in one direction. Trim pieced band to 42" long including seam allowances.

Diagram 11

3. Sew sashing strips to long edges of pieced band to make pillowcase border. Press seams toward sashing.

Assemble Pillowcase

1. Sew together pillowcase border and 42×22¼" and 42×7½" rectangles to make a pillowcase unit (**Diagram 12**). Press seams toward pillowcase border.

Diagram 12

2. Fold pillowcase unit in half, right sides together. Sew along long raw edge and short, unpieced edge of pillowcase unit. Turn right side out and press.

3. Fold raw edge of pillowcase unit under ¼" and press. Fold under again 3½"; press. Topstitch on right side to complete pillowcase.

Cabin
Tracks

*Designer Judy Hasheider created this quilt after examining an antique quilt
assembled using the Courthouse Steps method.*

Materials
1⅓ yards solid black (blocks, inner border, binding)

38—⅜-yard pieces assorted brown, gold, tan, red,
green, and black prints (blocks, sashing, borders)

½ yard bright green print (sashing)

5 yards backing fabric

71×90" batting

Finished quilt: 65×84"
Finished block: 7½" square

Quantities are for 44/45"-wide, 100% cotton fabrics.
Measurements include ¼" seam allowances. Sew
with right sides together unless otherwise stated.

General Assembly Tips
The blocks for this quilt are pieced using the
Courthouse Steps assembly method—sewing
matching rectangles to opposite edges of a center
square. All center squares are solid black.

Cut and Assemble Block A
The following instructions result in one Block A.
Repeat the cutting and assembly steps to make 13
total of Block A.

From solid black, cut:
- 1—2½" square

From one assorted print, cut:
- 2—1⅛×3¾" rectangles
- 2—1⅛×2½" rectangles

From a second assorted print, cut:
- 2—1⅜×5½" rectangles
- 2—1⅜×3¾" rectangles

From a third assorted print, cut:
- 2—1¼×7" rectangles
- 2—1¼×5½" rectangles

From a fourth assorted print, cut:
- 2—1×8" rectangles
- 2—1×7" rectangles

1. Sew 1⅛×2½" rectangles to opposite
edges of solid black 2½" square
(**Diagram 1**). Join 1⅛×3¾" rectangles to
remaining edges. Press all seams away
from center square.

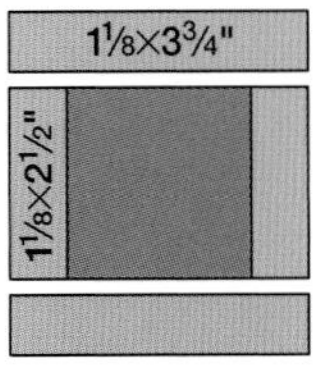

2. Sew 1⅜×3¾" rectangles to opposite
edges of Step 1 unit (**Diagram 2**). Join
1⅜×5½" rectangles to remaining edges.
Press all seams away from center.
continued

Diagram 1

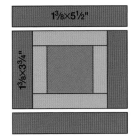

Diagram 2

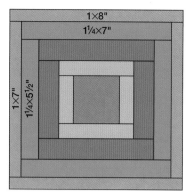

Diagram 3
Block A

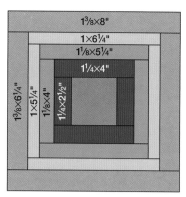

Diagram 4
Block B

3. Referring to **Diagram 3**, sew 1¼×5½" rectangles to opposite edges of Step 2 unit. Join 1¼×7" rectangles to remaining edges. Press all seams away from center.

4. Join 1×7" rectangles to opposite edges of Step 3 unit. Join 1×8" rectangles to remaining edges to complete Block A. Press all seams away from center. Block A should be 8" square including seam allowances.

Cut and Assemble Block B

Follow cutting instructions below and assembly method used for Block A to make one Block B; refer to **Diagram 4** for the order in which to add rectangles. Repeat to make 11 total of Block B.

From solid black, cut:
• 1—2½" square
From one assorted print, cut:
• 2—1¼×4" rectangles
• 2—1¼×2½" rectangles
From a second assorted print, cut:
• 2—1⅛×5¼" rectangles
• 2—1⅛×4" rectangles
From a third assorted print, cut:
• 2—1×6¼" rectangles
• 2—1×5¼" rectangles
From a fourth assorted print, cut:
• 2—1⅜×8" rectangles
• 2—1⅜×6¼" rectangles

Cut and Assemble Block C

Follow cutting instructions below and assembly method used for Block A to make one Block C; refer to **Diagram 5** for the order in which to add rectangles. Repeat to make 11 total of Block C.

From solid black, cut:
• 1—2½" square
From one assorted print, cut:
• 2—1×3½" rectangles
• 2—1×2½" rectangles
From a second assorted print, cut:
• 2—1¼×5" rectangles
• 2—1¼×3½" rectangles
From a third assorted print, cut:
• 2—1⅛×6¼" rectangles
• 2—1⅛×5" rectangles
From a fourth assorted print, cut:
• 2—1⅜×8" rectangles
• 2—1⅜×6¼" rectangles

Cut and Assemble Block D

Follow cutting instructions below and assembly method used for Block A to make one Block D; refer to **Diagram 6** for the order in which to add rectangles. Repeat to make 13 total of Block D.

From solid black, cut:
• 1—2½" square
From one assorted print, cut:
• 2—1⅜×4¼" rectangles
• 2—1⅜×2½" rectangles
From a second assorted print, cut:
• 2—1×5¼" rectangles
• 2—1×4¼" rectangles
From a third assorted print, cut:
• 2—1¼×6¾" rectangles
• 2—1¼×5¼" rectangles

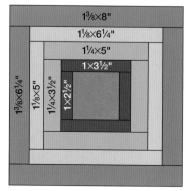

Diagram 5
Block C

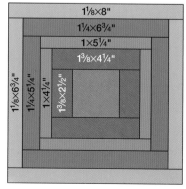

Diagram 6
Block D

Cabin Tracks

From a fourth assorted print, cut:
- 2—1⅛×8" rectangles
- 2—1⅛×6¾" rectangles

Assemble Quilt Center

From remaining assorted prints, cut:
- 165—1×22" strips

From bright green print, cut:
- 35—2½" sashing squares

1. Referring to **Diagram 7**, sew together 15 assorted print 1×22" strips to make a strip set. (Be sure to use a scant ¼" seam when joining strips; the finished strip set should be 8" tall including seam allowances.) Press seams in one direction. Repeat to make 11 strip sets total.

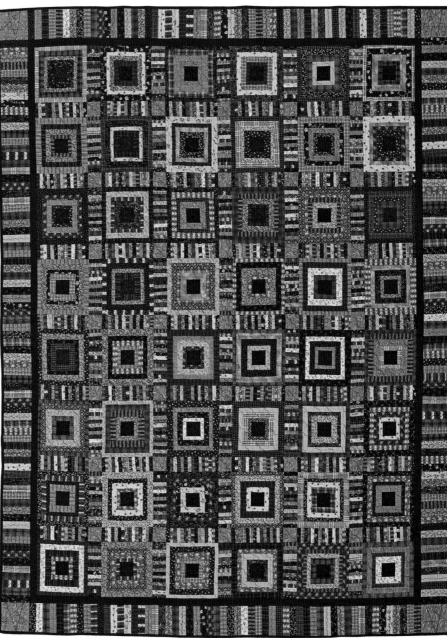

Diagram 7

2. Cut strip sets into 2½"-wide segments to make 82—2½×8" sashing strips total.

3. Referring to **Quilt Assembly Diagram** on *page 114*, lay out blocks, sashing strips, and sashing squares in 15 horizontal rows. Sew together pieces in each row. Press seams toward blocks and sashing squares.

4. Join rows to make quilt center. Press seams in one direction. The quilt center should be 55½×74½" including seam allowances.

continued

Cabin Tracks

Quilt Assembly Diagram

Assemble and Add Borders

From solid black, cut:
* 7—1½×42" strips

From remaining assorted prints, cut:
* 60—1½×22" strips

From bright green print, cut:
* 4—4¼" squares

1. Cut and piece solid black 1½×42" strips to make:
  * 2—1½×74½" inner border strips
  * 2—1½×57½" inner border strips

2. Sew long inner border strips to long edges of quilt center. Join short inner border strips to remaining edges. Press all seams toward border.

3. Sew together 15 assorted print 1½×22" strips to make a strip set. Press seams in one direction. Repeat to make four strip sets total.

4. Cut strip sets into 4¼"-wide segments to make 18 border segments total.

5. Sew together four border segments to make a short outer border unit. Press seams in one direction. Remove three of the 1½"-wide strips so the short outer border unit has 57 strips and measures 4¼×57½" including seam allowances. Reserve excess strips for long outer borders. Repeat to make a second short outer border unit.

6. Sew short outer border units to short edges of quilt center. Press seams toward outer border.

7. Sew together five border segments to make a long outer border unit. Press seams in one direction. Sew a reserved 1½"-wide strip to one end of long outer border unit so that it has 76 strips and measures 4¼×76½" including seam allowances. Repeat to make a second long outer border unit.

8. Sew a bright green print 4¼" square to each end of long outer border units. Sew long outer border units to remaining edges to complete quilt top. Press seams toward outer border.

Finish Quilt

From solid black, cut:
* 8—2½×42" binding strips

1. Layer quilt top, batting, and backing; baste. (For details, see Complete the Quilt, *page 159*.)

2. Quilt as desired. The machine-quilter stitched a star in the center of each bright green border square and in each block center. Diagonal wavy lines are stitched across the quilt and through the center of each strip in the outer border.

3. Bind with solid black binding strips. (For details, see Complete the Quilt.)

SHABBY CHIC THROW

Uniform placement of lights and darks creates dramatic contrast.

Materials

¼ yard beige dot (blocks)

8—⅛-yard pieces assorted pink prints (blocks)

9—¼-yard pieces assorted beige prints (blocks)

8—⅛-yard pieces assorted blue prints (blocks)

4—⅛-yard pieces *each* of assorted green and brown prints (blocks)

¼ yard red print (inner border)

1⅝ yards multicolor large floral (outer border, binding)

3½ yards backing fabric

61×76" batting

Finished quilt: 54½×69½"

Cut Fabrics and Assemble Blocks

The following instructions result in one pink block. Repeat cutting and assembly instructions to make 18 pink blocks total. Repeat using assorted beige and blue prints to make 15 blue blocks total. Repeat using assorted beige, green, and brown prints to make 15 green-and-brown blocks total.

From beige dot, cut:
• 1—2½" square
From *each* of one assorted pink print and one assorted beige print, cut:
• 1—1¼×4" rectangle
• 1—1¼×2½" rectangle
From *each* of a second assorted pink print and a second assorted beige print, cut:
• 1—1⅛×5¼" rectangle
• 1—1⅛×4" rectangle
From *each* of a third assorted pink print and a third assorted beige print, cut:
• 1—1×6¼" rectangle
• 1—1×5¼" rectangle
From *each* of a fourth assorted pink print and a fourth assorted beige print, cut:
• 1—1⅜×8" rectangle
• 1—1⅜×6¼" rectangle

1. Referring to **Diagram 8**, join pink print and beige print 1¼×2½" rectangles to opposite edges of beige dot 2½" square. Press seams toward rectangles. Sew pink print and beige print 1¼×4" rectangles to remaining edges; press seams away from center.

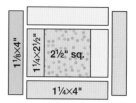

Diagram 8

2. In the same manner, continue adding rectangles to opposite edges of Step 1 unit to make a pink block (**Diagram 9**). The block should be 8" square including seam allowances.

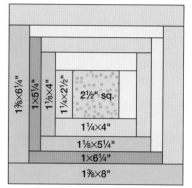

Diagram 9

Assemble Quilt Center

Referring to photo *opposite*, lay out blocks in eight horizontal rows. Join blocks in each row. Press seams in one direction, alternating direction with each row. Join rows to make quilt center. Press seams in one direction. The quilt center should be 45½×60½" including seam allowances.

Add Borders

From red print, cut:
• 6—1×42" strips for inner border
From multicolor large floral, cut:
• 7—4½×42" strips for outer border

1. Cut and piece red print 1×42" strips to make:
• 2—1×60½" inner border strips
• 2—1×46½" inner border strips

2. Sew long inner border strips to long edges of quilt center. Sew short inner border strips to remaining edges. Press seams toward inner border.

3. Cut and piece multicolor large floral 4½×42" strips to make:

- 2—4½×61½" outer border strips
- 2—4½×54½" outer border strips

4. Sew long outer border strips to long edges of quilt center. Join short outer border strips to remaining edges to complete quilt top. Press all seams toward outer border.

Finish Quilt

From multicolor large floral, cut:

- 7—2½×42" binding strips

1. Layer quilt top, batting, and backing; baste. (For details, see Complete the Quilt, *page 159*.)

2. Quilt as desired. This quilt was machine-quilted with an allover swirl design.

3. Bind with multicolor large floral binding strips. (For details, see Complete the Quilt.)

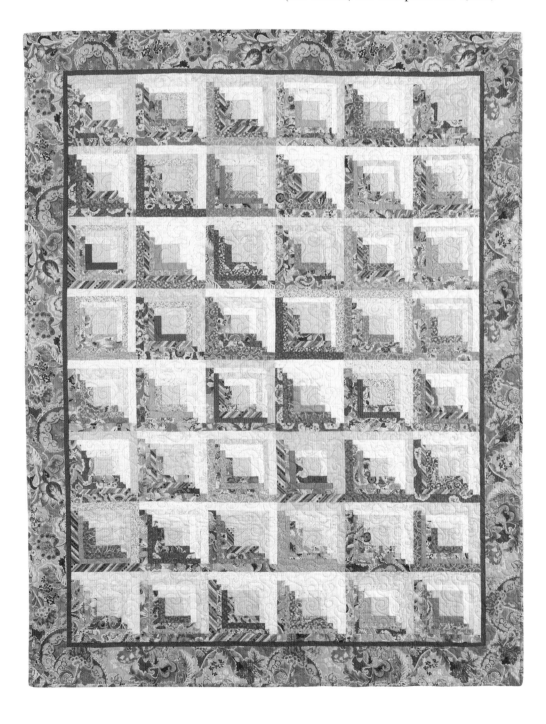

Cabin Tracks

ROMAN STRIPE WALL HANGING

Got scraps? Put those bits and pieces to use in a simple yet elegant quilt.

Materials

31—1×22" strips assorted metallic prints (pieced rows)

⅓ yard mottled red metallic (sashing)

⅝ yard red-and-metallic-gold print (border)

5—9×22" pieces (fat eighths) assorted metallic batiks (binding)

1 yard backing fabric

32×38" batting

Finished quilt: 26×32"

Cut Fabrics

Cut pieces in the following order.

From one assorted metallic print strip, cut:
- 4—1×2½" rectangles

From mottled red metallic, cut:
- 3—3½×23½" sashing strips

From red-and-metallic-gold print, cut:
- 2—4¾×33" border strips
- 2—4¾×27" border strips

From *each* metallic batik, cut:
- 12—2½" squares

Assemble Quilt Top

1. Referring to Assemble Quilt Center, *page 113,* steps 1 and 2, use 30 assorted metallic print 1×22" strips to make two strip sets. Cut strip sets into 2½"-wide segments to make 12—2½×8" segments total.

2. Referring to photo *opposite,* join three segments and one metallic print 1×2½" rectangle to make a 2½×23½" pieced row. Press seams in one direction. Repeat to make four pieced rows total.

3. Referring to photo, join pieced rows and sashing strips to make quilt center. Press seams toward sashing. The quilt center should be 17½×23½" including seam allowances.

4. With midpoints aligned, sew short border strips to short edges of quilt center, beginning and ending seams ¼" from corners. Add long border strips to remaining edges, mitering corners, to complete quilt top. (For details, see Mitered Border Corners, *page 157.*) Press all seams toward border.

Finish Quilt

1. Layer quilt top, batting, and backing; baste. (For details, see Complete the Quilt, *page 159.*)

2. Quilt as desired. This quilt features quilting in the ditch between the pieced rows and sashing. Each sashing strip is quilted with five vertical, parallel lines about ½" apart. The border contains a floral motif.

3. Join assorted metallic batik 2½" squares to make a pieced binding strip. Bind quilt with pieced binding strip. (For details, see Complete the Quilt.)

BIG-BLOCK
Beauty

Inspiration often comes in the most unlikely forms. Crates of tomatoes at designer Pat Sloan's local farmer's market inspired this quilt's robust color scheme.

Materials

¾ yard total assorted orange prints (blocks)

2⅔ yards total assorted green prints (blocks, sashing, binding)

1½ yards total assorted yellow prints (blocks)

1½ yards total assorted red prints (blocks)

⅝ yard green-and-orange stripe (inner border)

2½ yards red floral (outer border)

7⅞ yards backing fabric

94" square batting

Finished quilt: 87½" square
Finished block: 18" square
For additional quilt sizes, see Optional Sizes chart on Pattern Sheet 1.

Quantities are for 44/45"-wide, 100% cotton fabrics. Measurements include ¼" seam allowances. Sew with right sides together unless otherwise stated.

Cut Fabrics

Cut pieces in the following order. Cut outer border strips lengthwise (parallel to the selvages).

From assorted orange prints, cut:
- 11—2×42" strips

From assorted green prints, cut:
- Enough 2½"-wide strips in lengths ranging from 17" to 42" to total 400" for binding
- 11—2×42" strips
- 18—2×21½" sashing strips
- 18—2×18½" sashing strips

From assorted yellow prints, cut:
- 108—3⅞" squares

From assorted red prints, cut:
- 108—3⅞" squares

From green-and-orange stripe, cut:
- 7—2½×42" strips for inner border

From red floral, cut:
- 2—10½×87½" outer border strips
- 2—10½×67½" outer border strips

Assemble Blocks

1. Sew together an orange print 2×42" strip and a green print 2×42" strip to make a strip set. Press seam toward green print strip. Repeat to make 11 strip sets total. Cut strip sets into 216 2"-wide segments total (**Diagram 1**).

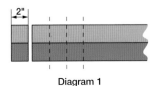

2"

Diagram 1

continued

5. Cut each pair apart on drawn line to make two triangle units (**Diagram 3**). Open triangle units; press seams toward red print triangles to make 216 triangle-squares total. Each triangle-square should be 3½" square including seam allowances.

6. Referring to **Diagram 4**, lay out 12 Four-Patch units and 24 triangle-squares in six rows; note rotation of seams in triangle-squares. Sew together pieces in each row. Press seams in one direction, alternating direction with each row. Join rows to make a block. Press seams in one direction. The block should be 18½" square including seam allowances. Repeat to make nine blocks total.

Diagram 4

7. Sew assorted green print 2×18½" sashing strips to opposite edges of a block. Add assorted green print 2×21½" sashing strips to remaining edges. Press all seams toward sashing strips. Repeat to add sashing to each block.

Assemble Quilt Center

1. Referring to photo *above left*, sew together blocks in three rows. Press seams in one direction, alternating direction with each row.

2. Join rows to make quilt center. Press seams in one direction. The quilt center should be 63½" square including seam allowances.

2. Referring to **Diagram 2**, join two 2"-wide segments to make a Four-Patch unit. Press seam in one direction. The unit should be 3½" square including seam allowances. Repeat to make 108 Four-Patch units total.

Diagram 2

3. Use a pencil to mark a diagonal line on wrong side of each yellow print 3⅞" square.

4. Layer a marked yellow print square atop each red print 3⅞" square. Sew each pair together with two seams, stitching ¼" on each side of drawn line (**Diagram 3**).

Diagram 3

Add Borders

I. Cut and piece green-and-orange stripe 2½×42" strips to make:
- 2—2½×67½" inner border strips
- 2—2½×63½" inner border strips

2. Sew short inner border strips to opposite edges of quilt center. Sew long inner border strips to remaining edges. Press all seams toward inner border.

3. Sew short outer border strips to opposite edges of quilt center. Sew long outer border strips to remaining edges to complete quilt top. Press all seams toward outer border.

Finish Quilt

I. Layer quilt top, batting, and backing; baste. (For details, see Complete the Quilt, *page 159.*)

2. Quilt as desired. Designer Pat Sloan free-motion-quilted a swirl design that reinforces the X shape in each block. In each sashing strip and inner border, she stitched a wave design. A large meandering leaf design accents the outer border (**Quilting Diagram**).

3. Using diagonal seams, join assorted green print 2½"-wide strips to make a pieced binding strip. Bind with pieced binding strip. (For details, see Complete the Quilt.)

Quilting Diagram

optional colors

Saddle Up and Ride Into the Night

What cowboy or cowgirl wouldn't like quilt tester Laura Boehnke's western-theme version of *Big-Block Beauty?* She used bandana and cowboy novelty prints for the large single-block pillow.

To make a 25"-square floor pillow, add sashing to one block, surround it with a 2"-wide-finished border, and sew on a backing. Stuff with fiberfill or insert a Euro-size pillow form.

THREE-BLOCK TABLE RUNNER

Big blocks make a bold statement on this quick-to-make runner.

Materials

3—⅛-yard pieces assorted brown prints (blocks)

3—⅛-yard pieces assorted olive green prints (blocks)

3—¼-yard pieces assorted beige prints (blocks)

¼ yard *each* light plum print, plum print, and plum check (blocks)

⅜ yard mottled black (sashing, inner border)

1½ yards plum floral (outer border, binding)

2¼ yards backing fabric

37×76" batting

Finished table runner: 31×70"

Cut Fabrics

Cut pieces in the following order.

From *each* brown print and *each* olive green print, cut:
• 2—2×42" strips

From *each* beige print, cut:
• 12—3⅞" squares

From light plum print, cut:
• 12—3⅞" squares

From plum print, cut:
• 12—3⅞" squares

From plum check, cut:
• 12—3⅞" squares

From mottled black, cut:
• 4—2×42" strips for inner border
• 2—2×18½" sashing strips

From plum floral, cut:
• 5—5¼×42" strips for outer border
• 6—2½×42" binding strips

Assemble Blocks

1. Referring to Assemble Blocks, *page 121*, steps 1 and 2, use brown print and olive green print 2×42" strips to make three sets of 12 matching Four-Patch units.

2. Referring to Assemble Blocks, steps 3 through 5, use eight 3⅞" squares from one beige print and eight light plum print 3⅞" squares to make 16 triangle-squares. Use four squares from the same beige print and four plum print 3⅞" squares to make eight additional triangle-squares.

3. Referring to Assemble Blocks, Step 6, and photo *below*, use 24 Step 2 triangle-squares and 12 matching Four-Patch units to make block A.

4. Repeat Step 2 using four squares from a second beige print and remaining light plum print squares to make eight triangle-squares. Repeat Step 2 using eight squares from the second beige print and eight plum check squares to make 16 triangle-squares.

5. Repeat Step 3 using Step 4 triangle-squares and 12 matching Four-Patch units to make block B.

6. Repeat Step 2 using eight squares from a third beige print and remaining plum print squares to make 16 triangle-squares. Repeat Step 2 using four squares from the third beige print and remaining plum check squares to make eight triangle-squares.

7. Repeat Step 3 using Step 6 triangle-squares and remaining matching Four-Patch units to make block C.

Assemble Table Runner Top

1. Referring to photo *below*, sew together blocks and sashing strips to make table runner center. Press seams toward sashing. The table runner center should be 18½×57½" including seam allowances.

2. Cut and piece mottled black 2×42" strips to make:
- 2—2×57½" inner border strips
- 2—2×21½" inner border strips

3. Sew long inner border strips to long edges of table runner center. Add short inner border strips to remaining edges. Press seams toward inner border.

4. Cut and piece plum floral 5¼×42" strips to make:
- 2—5¼×60½" outer border strips
- 2—5¼×31" outer border strips

5. Sew long outer border strips to long edges of table runner center. Add short outer border strips to remaining edges to complete table runner top. Press all seams toward outer border.

Finish Table Runner

1. Layer table runner top, batting, and backing; baste. (For details, see Complete the Quilt, *page 159*.)

2. Quilt as desired. Straight lines are machine-quilted in the triangle-squares, sashing, and inner border of this quilt. The Four-Patch units feature quilted circles, and the outer border contains a diamond grid.

3. Bind with plum floral binding strips. (For details, see Complete the Quilt.)

MESSENGER BAG

Show off your patchwork skills on a bag big enough to carry projects and notions.

Materials

18×22" (fat quarter) teal print (bag front)

18×22" (fat quarter) multicolor polka dot (bag front)

⅞ yard green print (bag front, binding)

1¼ yards beige print (bag front, back, bottom, and sides; strap)

⅝ yard dark green print (bag lining)

¾ yard heavy flannel (interlining)

1¾"-diameter ivory disc pendant bead

Finished bag: 18×18×3"

Cut Fabrics

Cut pieces in the following order.

From teal print, cut:
• 3—2×22" strips

From multicolor polka dot, cut:
• 3—2×22" strips

From green print, cut:
• 6—2½×42" binding strips
• 12—3⅞" squares

From beige print, cut:
• 4—3½×38½" strips
• 1—18½" square
• 2—3½×17" strips
• 12—3⅞" squares

From dark green print, cut:
• 2—18½" squares

From flannel, cut:
• 2—3½×38½" strips
• 2—18½" squares
• 1—3½×17" strip

Assemble Block

1. Referring to Assemble Blocks, *page 121*, steps 1 and 2, use teal print and multicolor polka dot strips to make 12 Four-Patch units total.

2. Referring to Assemble Blocks, steps 3 through 5, use green print and beige print squares to make 24 triangle-squares total.

3. Referring to Assemble Blocks, Step 6, and photo *opposite*, make one block.

Assemble Bag

1. With wrong sides together, layer the block and a dark green print 18½" square with a flannel 18½" square in between; baste around all edges to make bag front. Repeat to make bag back, using beige print 18½" square instead of the block.

2. Bind upper edge of bag front with green print binding strips. (For details, see Complete the Quilt,

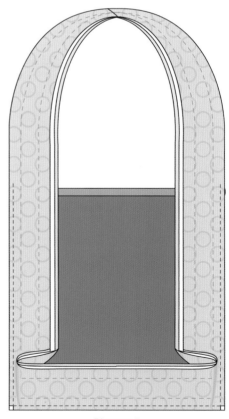

Diagram 5

page 159.) Repeat to bind upper edge of bag back.

3. Join short edges of two beige print 3½×38½" strips and one beige print 3½×17" strip to make a continuous outer loop for strap, bag sides, and bag bottom; press seams open. Repeat to make a lining loop. Repeat with flannel 3½×38½" strips and flannel 3½×17" strip to make an interlining loop.

4. Layer outer, interlining, and lining loops; baste. Machine-stitch 1" from each edge through all layers to make strap.

5. With lining sides together and raw edges aligned, sew strap to bag front lower edge, beginning and ending ¼" from each corner (**Diagram 5**; raw edges will be covered later with binding). Clip into strap at corners and continue sewing strap to each side edge of bag front, beginning ¼" from each lower corner and stitching past bag front upper edge.

6. Repeat Step 5, joining remaining raw edge of strap to bag back; do not catch bag front in stitching.

7. Use green print binding strips to bind edges of bag and strap. (For details, see Complete the Quilt.)

8. Sew bead onto center of bag front.

ADDICTED TO
APPLIQUÉ

If you're passionate about appliqué, you've probably

found a method that you love, but perhaps you're

still eager to experiment. If you're new to it, there

are options galore to explore. The pages that follow

showcase myriad ways to appliqué—needle-turn,

fusible, machine, and ragged-edge. Try them all

or adapt the method that works best for you to

complete the projects in this chapter.

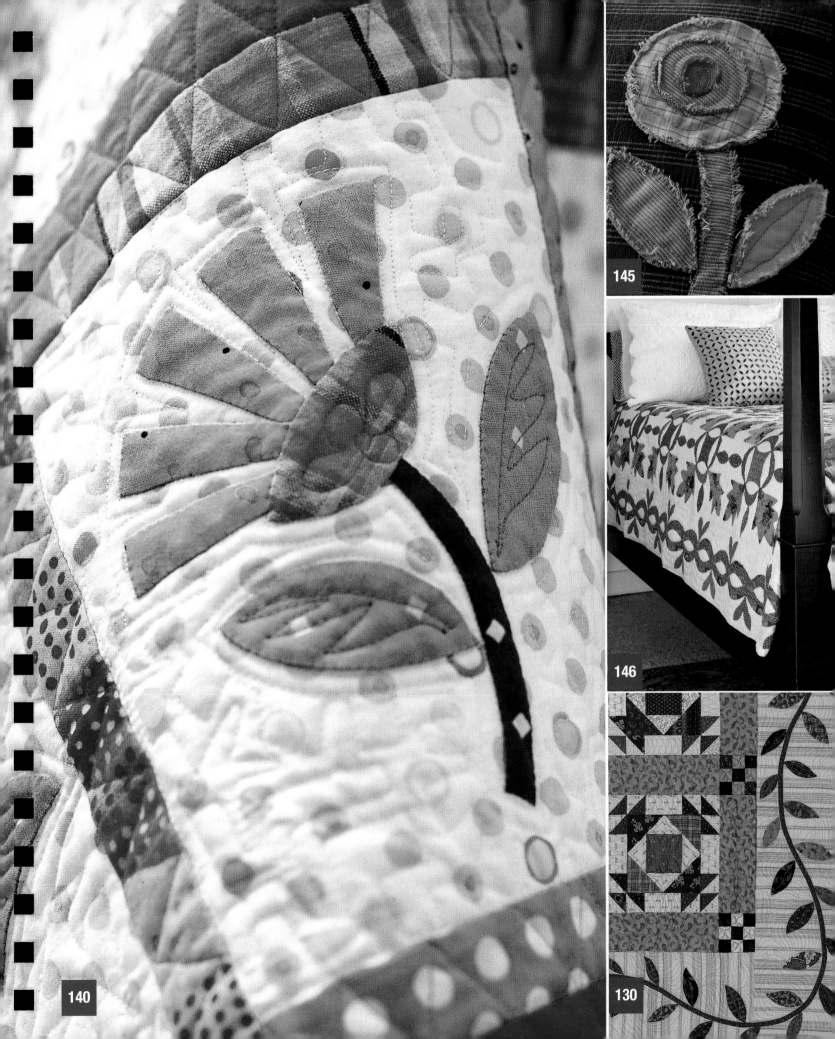

145

146

130

140

PRAIRIE *Vine*

Inspired by a passion for antique quilts and vintage-looking fabrics, designer Debbie Roberts beautifully blends patchwork and appliqué in an heirloom quilt.

Materials

1¼ yards gray-blue print (sashing)

2 yards green stripe (border)

½ yard dark brown print (vine appliqué)

⅝ yard brown print (binding)

14—9×22" pieces (fat eighths) assorted light prints in tan, ecru, and gold (blocks, sashing)

2¼ yards total assorted medium to dark prints in teal, brown, black, green, and rust (blocks, sashing, leaf appliqués)

4⅛ yards backing fabric

73" square batting

Finished quilt: 66½" square
Finished block: 9" square

Quantities are for 44/45"-wide, 100% cotton fabrics. Measurements include ¼" seam allowances. Sew with right sides together unless otherwise stated.

Cut Fabrics

Cut pieces in the order that follows in each section. The materials list includes extra yardage of green stripe for matching stripes in border.

From gray-blue print, cut:
- 40—3½×9½" sashing rectangles

From green stripe, cut:
- 7—8×42" strips for border

From dark brown print, cut:
- Enough 1¼"-wide bias strips to total 300" for vine appliqué (For details, see Cutting Bias Strips, *page 155*.) Designer Debbie Roberts used a ⅜"-wide bias tape maker to prepare the vine appliqué; for that method, cut bias strips ¾" wide and follow manufacturer's instructions to prepare strips.

From brown print, cut:
- 7—2½×42" binding strips

Cut and Assemble Double X Blocks

In most Double X blocks, Debbie used one light print and five dark prints. For a more antique look, Debbie made a few blocks quite scrappy, using up to 14 different prints. If desired, follow her lead and mix up prints when cutting.

The following instructions result in one Double X block. Repeat cutting and assembly instructions to make 16 Double X blocks total.

From one light print, cut:
- 4—2×3½" rectangles
- 2—3" squares, cutting each in half diagonally for 4 large triangles total
- 6—2⅜" squares, cutting each in half diagonally for 12 small triangles total

continued

From one medium or dark print, cut:
• 1—3½" square

From second medium or dark print, cut:
• 1—3⅞" square, cutting it in half diagonally for
  2 large triangles total

From third medium or dark print, cut:
• 1—3⅞" square, cutting it in half diagonally for
  2 large triangles total

From fourth medium or dark print, cut:
• 3—2⅜" squares, cutting each in half diagonally for
  6 small triangles total

From fifth medium or dark print, cut:
• 3—2⅜" squares, cutting each in half diagonally for
  6 small triangles total

1. Sew light print large triangles to opposite
edges of the medium or dark print 3½" square
(**Diagram 1**). Press seams toward triangles. Join
light print large triangles to remaining edges of
medium or dark print square to make a Square-in-a-
Square unit. Press seams toward triangles. The unit
should be 4¾" square including seam allowances.

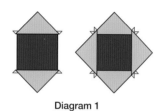

Diagram 1

2. Sew medium or dark print No. 2 large triangles
to opposite edges of Square-in-a-Square unit. Press
seams toward large triangles. Add medium or dark
print No. 3 large triangles to remaining edges to
make block center (**Diagram 2**). Press as before. The
block center should be 6½" square including seam
allowances.

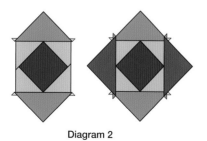

Diagram 2

3. Join a light print small triangle and a medium or
dark print No. 4 small triangle to make a triangle-
square (**Diagram 3**). Press seam toward medium or
dark print. The triangle-square should be 2" square
including seam allowances. Repeat to make six
triangle-squares total.

Diagram 3   Diagram 4

4. Using medium or dark print No. 5 small
triangles, repeat Step 3 to make six additional
triangle-squares (**Diagram 4**).

5. Referring to **Diagram 5**, lay out triangle-squares,
light print 2×3½" rectangles, and block center. Join
pieces in each side section; press seams toward light
print rectangles. Then add side sections to block
center; press seams toward side sections.

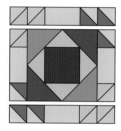

Diagram 5

6. Join pieces in top and bottom rows. Press seams
toward rectangles. Join rows to remaining edges of
block center to make a Double X block. Press seams
toward top and bottom rows. The block should be
9½" square including seam allowances.

Cut and Assemble Nine-Patch Units

Debbie made most of her Nine-Patch units with one
light print and one or two medium to dark prints.
As with the Double X blocks, she added extra prints
in a few units to give the quilt a more scrappy,
antique look.

The following instructions result in one
Nine-Patch unit. Repeat cutting and assembly
instructions to make 25 Nine-Patch units total.

From one light print, cut:
• 4—1½" squares
From one medium or dark print, cut:
• 4—1½" squares
From second medium or dark print, cut:
• 1—1½" square

1. Referring to **Diagram 6**, lay out all 1½" squares in three rows.

Diagram 6

2. Sew together squares in each row. Press seams toward medium or dark prints.

3. Join rows to make a Nine-Patch unit. Press seams toward top and bottom rows. The unit should be 3½" square including seam allowances.

   To reduce bulk, Debbie clipped seam allowances up to stitching line ¼" from each seam intersection. Then she pressed center portion of seam allowances open so that resulting seam allowances look like a tiny Four-Patch at each seam intersection.

Assemble Quilt Center

1. Referring to photo *above* and **Quilt Assembly Diagram** on *page 134*, lay out Double X blocks, Nine-Patch units, and gray-blue print sashing rectangles in nine horizontal rows.

2. Sew together pieces in each row. Press seams toward sashing rectangles. Join rows to make quilt center. Press seams in one direction. The quilt center should be 51½" square including seam allowances.

Assemble and Add Border

1. Cut and piece green stripe 8×42" strips to make:
- 2—8×66½" border strips
- 2—8×51½" border strips

continued

Quilt Assembly Diagram

2. Sew short border strips to opposite edges of quilt center. Join long border strips to remaining edges to complete quilt top. Press all seams toward border.

Prepare Vine Appliqué

1. Piece dark brown print 1¼"-wide bias strips to make one 300"-long strip. Fold strip in half lengthwise with wrong side inside; press.

2. Sew together long edges, stitching a scant ¼" from edges (**Diagram 7**). Trim seam allowances to ⅛". Refold strip, centering seam in back, to make vine appliqué; press.

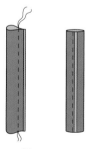

Diagram 7

Cut Leaf Appliqués and Appliqué Border

Patterns are on *Pattern Sheet 1*. To make templates of patterns, see Make and Use Templates, *page 155*.

From scraps of medium and dark prints, cut:
• 22 of Pattern A
• 9 of Pattern A reversed
• 29 of Pattern B
• 7 of Pattern C
• 10 of Pattern C reversed
• 26 of Pattern D
• 13 of Pattern D reversed
• 24 of Pattern E

1. Referring to **Quilt Assembly Diagram**, position vine appliqué in gentle curves around border; baste.

2. Using matching thread and a narrow zigzag stitch, machine-appliqué vine in place.

3. Arrange assorted medium and dark print A through E leaf appliqués along vine; baste.

4. Using thread that matches each appliqué, hand-appliqué leaves in place, turning under seam allowance with your needle as you stitch.

Finish Quilt

1. Layer quilt top, batting, and backing; baste. (For details, see Complete the Quilt, *page 159*.)

2. Quilt as desired. Machine-quilter Heidi Herring stitched a floral design in the block centers; she added feathers and meandering loops to accent the remaining areas of the blocks. She stitched feathers in the sashing and quilted around the appliquéd leaves in the border using a free-motion technique. A wavy line forms a vein in the center of each leaf.

3. Bind with brown print binding strips. (For details, see Complete the Quilt.)

optional colors

Fall Fun

Prints with a feeling of Arts and Crafts architecture are built into quilt tester Laura Boehnke's three-block table runner. "The earth-tone fabrics have such a subtle leaf motif that they could be used year-round," Laura says. "But they'll look especially great on my dining room table this fall." For a quick gift, consider using a novelty print for the sashing strips and choose coordinating solids or small prints to make the Double X blocks.

Laura liked the composition of this table runner so much that she made a second one from 1930s prints.

I SPY KID'S QUILT

Novelty prints are perfect for creating

a quilt of seek-and-find games.

Materials

18×22" piece (fat quarter) *each* light blue print, light yellow print, light orange print, blue dot, yellow dot, and orange dot (Nine-Patch units)

30—10" squares novelty prints (blocks)

⅓ yard *each* yellow, dark yellow, light blue, blue, dark blue, and light orange tone-on-tones (sashing)

½ yard *each* orange, red, and red-orange tone-on-tones (sashing)

2½ yards black dot (border, binding)

5¼ yards backing fabric

81×93" batting

Finished quilt: 75×87"

Cut Fabrics

Cut pieces in the following order.

From *each* light blue print, light orange print, and yellow dot, cut:

• 60—1½" squares

From *each* blue dot and orange dot, cut:

• 75—1½" squares

From light yellow print, cut:

• 48—1½" squares

From novelty prints, cut:

• 30—9½" squares

From *each* yellow, dark yellow, blue, and dark blue tone-on-tone, cut:

• 6—3½×9½" sashing rectangles

From *each* light blue and light orange tone-on-tone, cut:

• 8—3½×9½" sashing rectangles

From *each* orange and red tone-on-tone, cut:

• 10—3½×9½" sashing rectangles

From red-orange tone-on-tone, cut:

• 11—3½×9½" sashing rectangles

From black dot, cut:

• 9—6¼×42" strips for border
• 9—2½×42" binding strips

Assemble Nine-Patch Units

1. Referring to Cut and Assemble Nine-Patch Units, *page 132*, steps 1 through 3, and **Diagram 8**, use light blue print and blue dot 1½" squares to make a blue Nine-Patch unit. Repeat to make 15 blue Nine-Patch units total.

Diagram 8

2. Repeat Step 1 using light orange print and orange dot 1½" squares to make 15 orange Nine-Patch units total.

3. Repeat Step 1 using light yellow print and yellow dot 1½" squares to make 12 yellow Nine-Patch units total.

Assemble Quilt Center

1. Referring to photo at *right* for placement, lay out novelty print 9½" squares, sashing rectangles, and Nine-Patch units in 13 horizontal rows.

2. Sew together pieces in each row. Press seams toward sashing rectangles. Join rows to make quilt center; press seams in one direction. The quilt center should be 63½×75½" including seam allowances.

Add Border

1. Cut and piece black dot 6¼×42" strips to make:

• 2—6¼×75½" border strips
• 2—6¼×75" border strips

2. Sew long border strips to long edges of quilt center. Add short border strips to remaining edges to complete quilt top. Press seams toward border.

Finish Quilt

1. Layer quilt top, batting, and backing; baste. (For details, see Complete the Quilt, *page 159*.)

2. Quilt as desired. The featured quilt is machine-quilted with yellow thread in an allover swirl pattern.

3. Bind with black dot binding strips. (For details, see Complete the Quilt.)

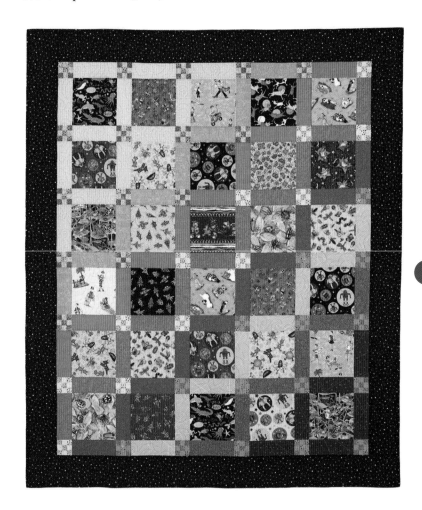

SPRING PLACE MATS & NAPKINS

Set a one-of-a-kind table by making your table linens.

Materials
for two place mats and napkins

12" square blue-and-green stripe (vine appliqués)

18×22" (fat quarter) *each* two blue prints and two lavender prints (leaf appliqués, napkins)

Scraps of assorted florals and checks in blue and lavender (leaf appliqués)

⅞ yard prequilted white fabric (place mat tops and backs)

Lightweight fusible web

Finished place mat: 18½×13½"
Finished napkin: 17" square

Cut Fabrics

Cut pieces in the following order. This project uses *Prairie Vine* patterns on *Pattern Sheet 1.* Place mats differ in leaf patterns used and color placement, although each has four blue and four lavender leaves.

To use fusible web for appliquéing, complete the following steps.

1. Lay fusible web, paper side up, over patterns. Use a pencil to trace each pattern the number of times indicated in cutting instructions, leaving ½" between tracings. Cut out each fusible-web shape roughly ¼" outside traced lines.

2. Following manufacturer's instructions, press each fusible-web shape onto wrong side of designated fabric; let cool. Cut out fabric shapes on drawn lines. Peel off paper backings.

From blue-and-green stripe, cut:
• 2—1¼×12½" bias strips (For details, see Cutting Bias Strips, *page 155.*)
From *each* blue print and lavender print, cut:
• 1—17½" square
From remaining blue and lavender prints and scraps of assorted florals and checks, cut:
• 4 *each* of patterns B and D
• 8 of Pattern C

From prequilted white fabric, cut:
• 4—19×14" rectangles

Appliqué and Assemble Place Mats

1. Referring to Prepare Vine Appliqué, *page 134*, use blue-and-green stripe bias strips to make two vine appliqués.

2. Referring to photo at *right*, position one vine and eight leaf appliqués on a prequilted white rectangle. When you are pleased with the arrangement, baste vine and fuse leaves in place.

3. Using thread to match each appliqué, machine-blanket-stitch around leaves and vine.

4. With right sides together, layer place mat top and prequilted white backing rectangle. Stitch around edges, leaving an opening for turning. Turn right side out; press. Whipstitch opening closed.

5. Machine-stitch 1" from edges, then 1⅛" from edges to complete place mat.

6. Repeat steps 2 through 5 to make a second place mat.

Assemble Napkins

With right sides together, layer blue print 17½" squares. Stitch around edges, leaving an opening for turning. Turn right side out; press. Whipstitch opening closed. Machine-stitch ⅞" and 1" from outer edges to complete napkin.

Repeat with lavender print 17½" squares to make a second napkin.

Garden
Blooms

A sampler of appliqué flowers from Piece O' Cake designers
Becky Goldsmith and Linda Jenkins lets you practice your needle-turn skills.

Materials

1⅛ yards white polka dot
  (appliqué foundations, border)

Assorted scraps brown and green prints (appliqués)

⅞ yard total assorted red and orange prints
  (appliqués, sashing, binding)

½ yard total assorted blue prints
  (appliqués, sashing, binding)

½ yard total assorted purple prints
  (appliqués, sashing, binding)

1 yard backing fabric

36×39" batting

⅓ yard clear upholstery vinyl or other clear
  flexible plastic (optional)

Finished quilt: 29½×32½"
Finished blocks: 7×8"

Quantities are for 44/45"-wide, 100% cotton fabrics.
Measurements include ¼" seam allowances. Sew
with right sides together unless otherwise stated.

Make Templates

Over the years, designers Becky Goldsmith and
Linda Jenkins have developed their own appliqué
method, which uses an overlay for placement
purposes. The following instructions are for their
overlay method.

1. Patterns are on *Pattern Sheet 2*. Accurately trace
all pattern pieces onto template plastic.

2. Cut out templates on drawn lines with sharp
scissors. Linda and Becky stress the importance of
keeping template edges smooth and points sharp.

3. Mark right side of each template with its letter
and number designation. Letters identify specific
pieces; numbers indicate order of appliquéing.

Cut Fabrics

Cut pieces in the following order. Appliqué
foundations are cut larger than necessary to allow
for sewing differences. You'll trim foundations to
correct size after appliquéing.

When tracing appliqué shapes, lay fabrics and
templates with right sides up; trace. Add a ³⁄₁₆" seam
allowance to all edges when cutting out appliqué
pieces.

From white polka dot, cut:
• 2—2½×32½" border strips
• 9—9×10" foundation rectangles
From assorted brown print scraps, cut:
• 3 *each* of patterns A, J, and R

continued

From assorted green print scraps, cut:
- 3 *each* of patterns H, I, K, L, P, and Q

From assorted red and orange prints, cut:
- Enough 2½"-wide strips in varying lengths to total 70" for binding
- 2—1½×32½" sashing strips
- 12—1½×7½" sashing rectangles
- 2 *each* of patterns B, C, D, E, F, O, S, and T
- 3 of Pattern G
- 1 of Pattern N

From assorted blue prints, cut:
- Enough 2½"-wide strips in varying lengths to total 35" for binding
- 1—1½×32½" sashing strip
- 6—1½×7½" sashing rectangles
- 1 *each* of patterns B, C, D, E, F, N, and O
- 2 of Pattern M

From assorted purple prints, cut:
- Enough 2½"-wide strips in varying lengths to total 45" for binding
- 1—1½×32½" sashing strip
- 6—1½×7½" sashing rectangles
- 1 *each* of patterns M, N, S, and T

From clear upholstery vinyl, cut:
- 3—7×8" rectangles

Appliqué Blocks

1. Lightly press each white polka dot 9×10" foundation rectangle in half horizontally and vertically to form placement lines; unfold.

2. Center and position a vinyl 7×8" rectangle over Garden Blooms Block A Full-Size Placement Diagram on *Pattern Sheet 2;* use a permanent marker to accurately trace design, including placement lines, letters, and numbers, to make a full-size overlay. (Extend placement lines to edges of vinyl overlay.)

3. Repeat Step 2 with remaining vinyl 7×8" rectangles to trace Garden Blooms Block B Full-Size Placement Diagram and Block C Full-Size Placement Diagram, both on *Pattern Sheet 2.*

4. Position Block A overlay on a creased foundation rectangle, aligning overlay's placement lines with pressed lines. Pin top of overlay to fabric, if desired.

5. Finger-press seam allowances under, then slide a brown print A stem piece right side up between foundation rectangle and overlay. Remove overlay, pin stem to foundation, and use matching thread to appliqué stem in place.

6. Use overlay to position the next piece in stitching sequence; pin and appliqué as before. Working in numerical order, continue in this manner—positioning pieces, removing overlay to pin them to foundation, and appliquéing them in place—to complete Block A (**Diagram 1**).

7. Press appliquéd block from back; trim it to 7½×8½" including seam allowances.

8. Repeat steps 4 through 7 to make three total of Block A, three of Block B (**Diagram 2**), and three of Block C (**Diagram 3**); always appliqué pieces in numerical order.

Assemble Quilt Top

1. Referring to **Quilt Assembly Diagram**, lay out appliquéd blocks; assorted red, orange, blue, and purple print sashing rectangles; and assorted red, orange, blue, and purple print sashing strips in seven vertical rows.

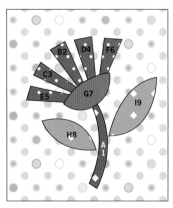

Block A
Diagram 1

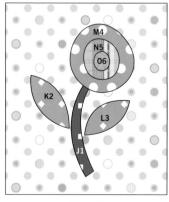

Block B
Diagram 2

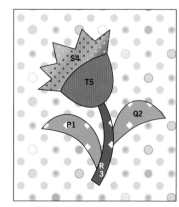

Block C
Diagram 3

2. Sew together pieces in each vertical block row. Press seams toward sashing rectangles. Join rows and sashing strips to make quilt center. Press seams toward sashing strips. The quilt center should be 25½×32½" including seam allowances.

3. Sew white polka dot 2½×32½" border strips to side edges of quilt center to complete quilt top.

Finish Quilt

1. Layer quilt top, batting, and backing; baste. (For details, see Complete the Quilt, *page 159.*) Quilt as desired.

2. Using diagonal seams, join assorted red, orange, blue, and purple print 2½"-wide strips to make a pieced binding strip. Bind with pieced binding strip. (For details, see Complete the Quilt.)

Quilt Assembly Diagram

Perfect Appliqué Every Time

"Learning to appliqué is like anything else. When you learn the tricks to doing it right, what looks difficult actually becomes very simple," says Linda Jenkins.

Follow the Piece O' Cake designers' appliqué tips for success.

1. Don't be shy when tracing around templates onto the fabrics. Draw a line that you can see. If your line is too faint, it is difficult to know where to turn the seam allowance under.

2. Finger-press your appliqué piece before pinning it to the block. Hold the appliqué piece right side up. Using your thumb and index finger, turn the seam allowance to the back of the appliqué so that the drawn line is just barely turned under. You don't want to see the drawn line on the top of your appliqué piece. Use your fingers to press a crease into the fabric along the inside of the drawn line.

3. Use two-ply, 50- or 60-weight, 100% cotton thread for hand appliqué. Match the color and value (light/medium/dark) of your thread to the appliqué fabric.

4. To make the stitch, hold the needle perpendicular to the appliqué foundation. The needle enters the appliqué foundation next to the appliqué, near where the last stitch came up out of the appliqué fabric. Push the needle through the background fabric. You'll feel the needle tip with your middle finger underneath the block. Your right hand falls to the right as you rock across your underneath finger. The needle tip comes up through the foundation and the edge of the appliqué piece to complete the stitch.

5. Stitch length is important. As in piecing, an ⅛" stitch is too long. A stitch that is ⁷⁄₁₆" is a little short in most places. The designers recommend 10 to 14 stitches per inch depending on the appliqué shape and the fabric type. Look at your appliqué as you sew. If it looks loose, shorten your stitch. Pull each stitch tight without pleating the fabric.

FRAMED FLOWERS

Fuse, stitch, and embellish a trio of flowers to showcase in purchased picture frames.

Materials

8×10" piece *each* yellow print, cream-and-green plaid, and cream print (appliqué foundations)

Scraps of assorted green prints (stem and leaf appliqués)

Scrap of black-and-red print (flower appliqués)

Scraps of assorted prints and solids in red, turquoise, and coral (flower appliqués)

Lightweight fusible web

Machine embroidery thread: yellow, green, black, and variegated

Assorted seed beads and bugle beads

3 assorted frames with 4×6" openings

Cut Fabrics

Cut pieces in the following order. This project uses *Garden Blooms* patterns on *Pattern Sheet 2*. To use fusible web for appliquéing, complete these steps.

1. Lay fusible web, paper side up, over patterns. Use a pencil to trace each pattern the number of times indicated in cutting instructions, leaving ½" between tracings. Cut out each fusible-web shape roughly ¼" outside traced lines.

2. Following manufacturer's instructions, press each fusible-web shape onto wrong side of designated fabric; let cool. Cut out fabric shapes on drawn lines. Peel off paper backings.

From assorted green prints, cut:
• 1 *each* of patterns J, K, P, and R reversed
From black-and-red print, cut:
• 1 *each* of patterns B, C, D, E, and F
From assorted red, turquoise, and coral prints and solids, cut:
• 1 *each* of patterns G, M, N, O, S, and T

Appliqué and Frame Blocks

1. Referring to photos *above left* and Framed Flowers Appliqué Placement Diagrams on *Pattern Sheet 2*, lay out appliqués on corresponding yellow print, cream-and-green plaid, and cream print foundations. Fuse in place.

2. For turquoise flower, use yellow thread to zigzag-stitch around each circle appliqué; straight-stitch with green thread inside edges of leaf and stem and through leaf center. For coral tulip, use variegated thread to featherstitch around flower, stem, and leaf appliqués. For black-and-red flower, machine-blanket-stitch with black thread around each petal appliqué. Lightly press from wrong side.

3. Hand-sew assorted seed beads and bugle beads onto appliqués and foundation as desired to complete each block.

4. Mount and insert each block into frame.

RAGGED-APPLIQUÉ PILLOW

Create blooms in no time with machine-appliquéd flowers made from layered fabric.

Materials

⅞ yard purple plaid (appliqué foundation, pillow back)

¼ yard total assorted green stripes and plaids (stem and leaf appliqués)

⅛ yard total assorted tan solids, stripes, and plaids (leaf and flower appliqués)

⅛ yard total assorted aqua solids and plaids (flower appliqués)

⅛ yard total assorted pink solids, stripes, and plaids (flower appliqués)

8" square light gold plaid (flower appliqué)

12" square solid gold (flower appliqué)

Fiberfill

Finished pillow: 30×12"

Cut Fabrics

Cut pieces in the following order. This project uses *Garden Blooms* patterns plus an additional pattern, Pattern U, on *Pattern Sheet 2*.

To make templates of patterns, see Make and Use Templates, *page 155*. Place templates *facedown on right side* of fabrics and do not add seam allowances when cutting appliqué shapes.

Each appliqué on the pillow is composed of a set of three identical shapes layered atop each other. To save time, layer fabrics and cut each set simultaneously. Keep each set pinned together; it will be stitched to foundation as one unit.

From purple plaid, cut:
- 1—32×14" rectangle
- 1—31×13" rectangle

From assorted green stripes and plaids, cut:
- 12 of Pattern J
- 6 of Pattern K
- 3 *each* of patterns L, Q, and R

From assorted tan solids, stripes, and plaids, cut:
- 9 of Pattern L
- 6 of Pattern K
- 3 *each* of patterns N, O, and P

From assorted aqua solids and plaids, cut:
- 6 of Pattern M
- 3 of Pattern N

From assorted pink solids, stripes, and plaids, cut:
- 6 *each* of patterns M and N
- 9 of Pattern O

From light gold plaid, cut:
- 3 of Pattern G

From solid gold, cut:
- 3 of Pattern U

Appliqué Pillow Top and Finish Pillow

1. Referring to Ragged-Appliqué Pillow Appliqué Placement Diagram on *Pattern Sheet 2*, lay out sets of flower, stem, and leaf appliqués on purple plaid 32×14" rectangle. Pin or baste in place.

2. Machine-straight-stitch a spiral on round flowers, beginning at outside edges and stitching to flower centers. Stitch ⅛" inside raw edges of remaining appliqués.

3. Trim purple plaid rectangle to 31×13" including seam allowances to complete pillow top.

4. With right sides together, layer pillow top and purple plaid 31×13" rectangle. Sew together with ½" seam allowance; leave an opening for turning.

5. Turn right side out; press. Stuff with fiberfill and whipstitch opening closed. Use a stiff brush to fray raw edges of appliqués.

MAJESTIC
Oak Reel

Practice makes perfect, especially when it comes to appliquéing sharp points and curves. Improve your hand-appliqué skills—one block at a time—by re-creating this vintage queen-size quilt from the collection of Kay Triplett.

Materials

10¼ yards solid cream or muslin (appliqué foundations, border, binding)

2⅜ yards total assorted red prints (block appliqués)

3⅞ yards green floral (block appliqués)

⅔ yard green print (border appliqués)

2⅞ yards red-and-blue stripe (border appliqués)

8½ yards backing fabric

101×108" batting

Freezer paper

Finished quilt: 95×102"
Finished block: 15½" square

Quantities are for 44/45"-wide, 100% cotton fabrics. Measurements include ¼" seam allowances. Sew with right sides together unless otherwise stated.

Cut Fabrics

Cut pieces in the following order. Cut continuous appliqué strips and border and binding strips lengthwise (parallel to the selvages). Border strip measurements allow extra length for mitering corners at bottom of quilt.

Patterns are on *Pattern Sheet 1*. To use freezer-paper templates for cutting appliqué shapes, complete the following steps.

1. Lay freezer paper, shiny side down, over patterns. Use a pencil to trace each pattern the number of times indicated in cutting instructions. Cut out freezer-paper shapes on traced lines. (Patterns F and G are connected at dotted lines to create a continuous appliqué strip for each border.)

2. Using a hot, dry iron, press each freezer-paper shape, shiny side down, onto right side of designated fabric; leave ½" between shapes. Let cool.

3. Cut out fabric shapes, adding a 3/16" seam allowance to all edges. Leave freezer paper in place. Clip inside curves or points on appliqués.

From solid cream, cut:
- 2—9×103" border strips
- 1—9×96" border strip
- 10—2½×42" binding strips
- 30—17" squares

From assorted red prints, cut:
- 30 sets of 9 matching pieces (1 of Pattern A and 4 *each* of patterns B and C)

From green floral, cut:
- 60 *each* of patterns D and D reversed

continued

Appliqué Blocks

1. Fold each solid cream 17" square in half diagonally twice. Lightly finger-press to create foundation squares with appliqué placement guidelines; unfold.

2. Referring to **Appliqué Placement Diagram**, lay out one red print A piece, four red print B pieces, and four red print C pieces on a foundation square. Add two green print D leaves and two green print D reversed leaves opposite each other, tucking ends of A and B pieces beneath leaves; baste in place.

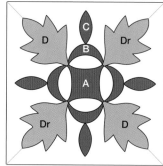

Appliqué Placement Diagram

3. Using threads that match appliqués, hand-appliqué pieces to foundation to make an appliquéd block. Use tip of needle to turn seam allowances under along freezer-paper edges as you stitch. Remove freezer-paper templates.

4. Repeat steps 2 and 3 to make 30 appliquéd blocks total.

5. Press each block from wrong side. With appliquéd designs centered, trim blocks to 16" square including seam allowances.

From green print, cut:
• 49 of Pattern E

From red-and-blue stripe, cut:
• 2 side border appliqué strips
  (To create a continuous appliqué strip, trace one of Pattern G, 15 of Pattern F, and one of Pattern G with point facing opposite direction.)
• 1 bottom border appliqué strip
  (To create a continuous appliqué strip, trace one of Pattern G, 13 of Pattern F, and one of Pattern G with point facing opposite direction.)

TIP: *When cutting appliqué foundations, stay at least ½" away from the selvage edge, which is tightly woven. The selvage can cause a foundation to have a rippled edge if it's incorporated.*

Assemble Quilt Center

1. Lay out appliquéd blocks in six rows (**Quilt Assembly Diagram**).

2. Sew together blocks in each row. Press seams in one direction, alternating direction with each row. Join rows to make quilt center. Press seams in one direction. The quilt center should be 78×93½" including seam allowances.

Add and Appliqué Border

1. With top edges aligned, sew solid cream 9×103" border strips to long edges of quilt center, ending seams ¼" from bottom corners. Add solid cream 9×96" border strip to bottom edge of quilt center, mitering corners, to complete quilt top. (For details, see Mitered Border Corners, *page 157*.) Press all seams toward border.

2. Referring to photo *opposite* and **Quilt Assembly Diagram**, place red-and-blue stripe border appliqué strips on side and bottom borders; note how strips meet at mitered seams. Baste strips in place.

3. Lay out green print E pieces along both sides of appliqué strips, noting placement in corners (there are two in one corner, one in the other); baste.

4. Using threads that match appliqués, hand-appliqué pieces to border.

Finish Quilt

1. Layer quilt top, batting, and backing; baste. (For details, see Complete the Quilt, *page 159*.)

2. Quilt as desired. Hand quilting on this antique quilt repeats the teardrop shapes and curves of the appliqués (**Quilting Diagram**). Echo quilting emphasizes the scallop design in the border. An X stitched through the center of each block offers a contrasting linear design and creates a center vein on each leaf.

3. Bind with solid cream binding strips. (For details, see Complete the Quilt.)

Quilt Assembly Diagram

QUILTING DIAGRAM

149

Majestic Oak Reel

continued

Chintz Fabric Enhances Quilt

Quiltmaker and antique quilt enthusiast Kay Triplett has been collecting quilts since her childhood, when she earned money mowing lawns to have tops quilted by her grandmother's quilting group.

"My collection is mostly red-and-green mid-19th century [quilts] and numbers about 500," Kay says. "The majority would be from the Pennsylvania area, and my favorites tend to be a little folksy, often bold and colorful."

When opportunity and budget allow, Kay purchases older quilts, even if they aren't red and green.

"I have quite a few late 1700s to early 1800s chintz quilts, and when I find a red-and-green chintz quilt, it's normally a must-have. I am also a sucker for elaborate quilting and have a few early quilts from Provence, France," she says.

To research the history of the block in *Majestic Oak Reel*, Kay turned to quilt designer and historian Terry Clothier Thompson's Web site (*terrythompson.com*). Kay learned this block was likely inspired by an oak leaf and reel design from about 1830 (a time when the reel shape was used as the center of many appliqué patterns). Kay purchased the quilt from a New England quilt dealer at the International Quilt Market in Houston about 15 years ago and dates the fabrics to the early to mid-19th century.

"The chintz fabric was likely imported and very expensive at the time," Kay says. "I do not have documentation, but I believe this is toward the early end of the known quilts of this pattern."

Kay is a member of the Quilt Guild of Greater Houston, the American Quilt Study Group, and The Woodlands Area Quilt Guild.

optional colors

Focus on Home Dec Fabrics

Try using home decorating fabrics in a quilt for dramatic change. For this table covering, quilt tester Laura Boehnke used a variety of fabric textures, including a tapestry print and sateen solids. Instead of needle-turn appliqué, she chose fusible web, a satin stitch, and complementary thread colors for a smooth, professional-looking finish.

"When appliquéing, remember to choose your needle and thread based on the fabric you're using," Laura says. Sewing on heavier fabrics may require a larger needle and a change in thread fiber. To produce uniform stitches, work slowly and sew at an even pace.

FRAMED WALL HANGING

A single block embellished with blanket stitching makes a striking picture.

Materials

22" square black felted wool (foundation)

6" square gold felted wool (appliqué)

8×10" piece blue felted wool (appliqués)

6×8" piece green felted wool (small leaf appliqués)

14" square rust felted wool (large leaf appliqués)

Embroidery floss: gold, blue, green, and rust

Freezer paper

Frame with 15½"-square opening

Finished picture (inside opening): 15½" square

Cut Fabrics

Cut pieces in the following order. This project uses *Majestic Oak Reel* patterns on *Pattern Sheet 1*.

To felt wool, machine-wash it in a hot-water-wash, cool-rinse cycle with a small amount of detergent; machine-dry on high heat and steam-press.

To use freezer paper for cutting appliqué shapes, complete the following steps.

I. Lay freezer paper, shiny side down, over patterns. Use a pencil to trace each pattern the number of times indicated in cutting instructions. Cut out freezer-paper shapes roughly ¼" outside drawn lines.

2. Using a hot, dry iron, press each freezer-paper shape, shiny side down, onto right side of designated fabric. Cut out fabric shapes on drawn lines. Peel off freezer paper.

From gold wool, cut:
- 1 of Pattern A

From blue wool, cut:
- 4 of Pattern B

From green wool, cut:
- 4 of Pattern C

From rust wool, cut:
- 4 of Pattern D

Appliqué Block

I. Referring to photo *above* and Appliqué Blocks, *page 148*, steps 1 and 2, baste appliqués onto black wool foundation square.

2. Using three strands of matching embroidery floss, blanket-stitch around each appliqué. To blanket-stitch, pull the needle up at A (**Blanket Stitch Diagram**), form a reverse L shape with the floss, and hold the angle of the L shape in place with your thumb. Push the needle down at B and come up at C to secure the stitch. Continue in the same manner.

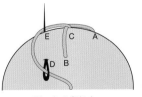

Blanket Stitch

Frame Block

Centering design, trim block to 17½" square. Mount and insert appliquéd piece into frame.

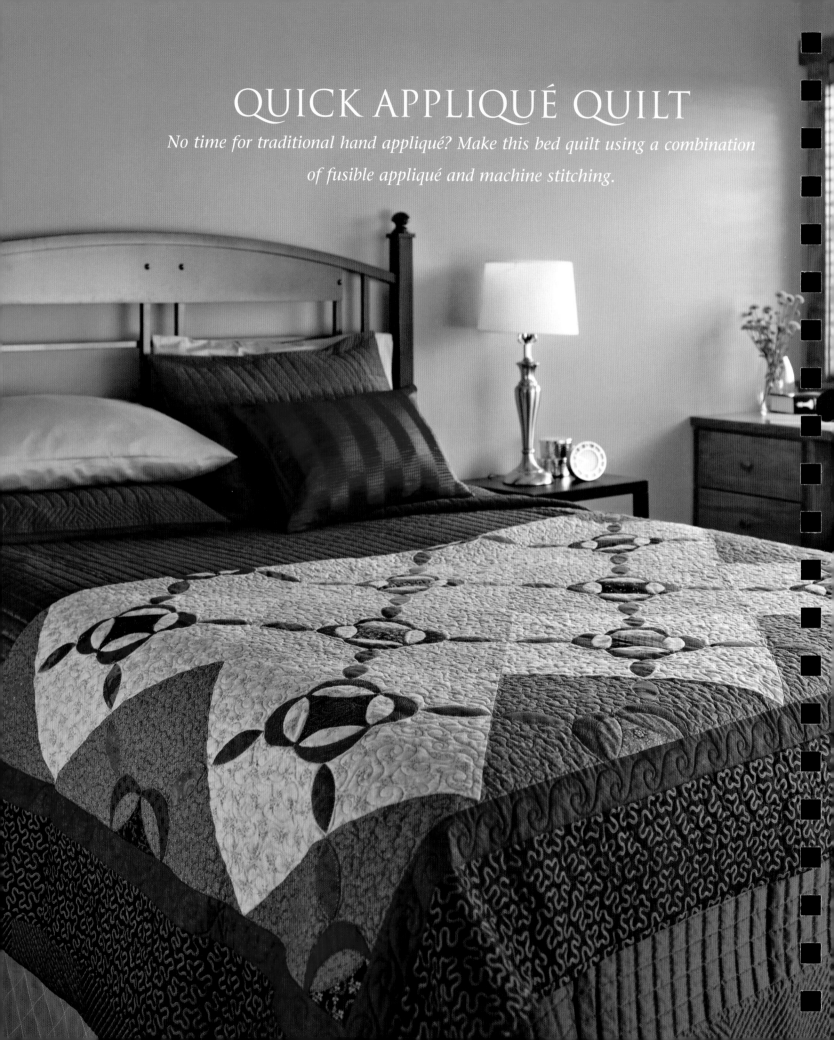

QUICK APPLIQUÉ QUILT

No time for traditional hand appliqué? Make this bed quilt using a combination of fusible appliqué and machine stitching.

Materials

2½ yards tan print No. 1 (appliqué foundations)

1 yard tan print No. 2 (appliqué foundations)

½ yard total assorted blue prints (appliqués)

⅝ yard total assorted red, rust, and brown prints (appliqués)

½ yard total assorted olive green prints (appliqués)

1⅜ yards brown-and-red print (setting and corner triangles)

⅝ yard rust tone-on-tone (inner border)

2⅓ yards navy blue print (outer border, binding)

7⅓ yards backing fabric

88" square batting

Lightweight fusible web

Finished quilt: 81¼" square

Cut Fabrics

Cut pieces in the following order. This project uses *Majestic Oak Reel* patterns on *Pattern Sheet 1.* To use fusible web for appliquéing, complete the following steps.

1. Lay fusible web, paper side up, over appliqué patterns. Use a pencil to trace patterns the number of times indicated in cutting instructions, leaving ½" between tracings. Cut out each fusible-web shape roughly ¼" outside traced lines.

2. Following manufacturer's instructions, press each fusible-web shape onto wrong side of designated fabric; let cool. Cut out fabric shapes on drawn lines. Peel off paper backings.

From tan print No. 1, cut:
• 9—17" squares
From tan print No. 2, cut:
• 4—17" squares
From assorted blue prints, cut:
• 25 of Pattern A
From assorted red, rust, and brown prints, cut:
• 72 of Pattern B (13 sets of 4 matching pieces, 8 sets of 2 matching pieces, and 4 assorted pieces)

From assorted olive green prints, cut:
• 72 of Pattern C (13 sets of 4 matching pieces and 20 assorted pieces)
From brown-and-red print, cut:
• 2—23¼" squares, cutting each diagonally twice in an X for 8 setting triangles total
• 2—11⅞" squares, cutting each in half diagonally for 4 corner triangles total
From rust tone-on-tone, cut:
• 7—2½×42" strips for inner border
From navy blue print, cut:
• 9—6×42" strips for outer border
• 9—2½×42" binding strips

Appliqué Blocks and Triangles

1. Referring to Appliqué Blocks, *page 148,* Step 1, prepare tan print No. 1 and No. 2—17" squares to create foundation squares with placement guidelines.

2. Referring to **Appliqué Placement Diagram**, *page 148* (omitting D pieces), lay out one A piece, four matching B pieces, and four matching C pieces on a foundation square; fuse in place. Using matching thread, machine-blanket-stitch pieces in place to make an appliquéd block. Repeat to make 13 appliquéd blocks total.

3. Referring to Appliqué Blocks, Step 5, press and trim each block.

4. Fold a setting triangle in half; finger-press to form a placement guideline. Referring to **Diagram 1**, lay out one A piece, two matching B pieces, and two assorted C pieces on triangle. Fuse in place. Trim edge of A piece even with long edge of triangle. Machine-blanket-stitch pieces as before to make an appliquéd setting triangle. Press triangle from wrong side. Repeat to make eight appliquéd setting triangles total.

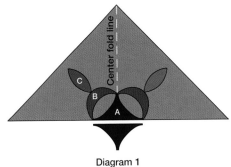

Diagram 1

continued

Assemble Quilt Center

1. Referring to photo at *left,* lay out appliquéd blocks and setting triangles in diagonal rows, alternating blocks with tan print No. 1 and No. 2 foundations. Sew together pieces in each row. Press seams in one direction, alternating direction with each row.

2. Join rows to make quilt center. Press seams in one direction. Add appliquéd corner triangles to complete quilt center. Press seams toward corner triangles. The quilt center should be 66¼" square including seam allowances.

Add Borders

1. Cut and piece rust tone-on-tone 2½×42" strips to make:
- 2—2½×70¼" inner border strips
- 2—2½×66¼" inner border strips

2. Join short inner border strips to opposite edges of quilt center. Add long inner border strips to remaining edges. Press all seams toward inner border.

3. Cut and piece navy blue print 6×42" strips to make:
- 2—6×81¼" outer border strips
- 2—6×70¼" outer border strips

4. Sew short outer border strips to opposite edges of quilt center. Add long outer border strips to remaining edges to complete quilt top. Press all seams toward outer border.

Finish Quilt

1. Layer quilt top, batting, and backing; baste. (For details, see Complete the Quilt, *page 159.*)

2. Quilt as desired. The featured quilt is stitched with a wave design in the block backgrounds and stippling in the triangle backgrounds. The wave motif is continued in the inner border, and a feather pattern is quilted in the outer border.

3. Bind with navy blue print binding strips. (For details, see Complete the Quilt.)

5. Fold a corner triangle in half; finger-press to form a placement guideline as before. Lay out one assorted A, B, and C piece on triangle; fuse in place (**Diagram 2**). Trim A piece even with short edges of triangle. Machine-blanket-stitch pieces as before to make an appliquéd corner triangle. Press triangle from wrong side. Repeat to make four appliquéd corner triangles total.

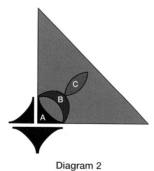

Diagram 2

QUILTER'S SCHOOLHOUSE

Refer to these tips and techniques when making your projects.

CHOOSE FABRICS

The best fabric for quiltmaking is 100% cotton because it minimizes seam distortion, presses crisply, and is easy to quilt. Unless otherwise noted, quantities in Materials lists are for 44/45"-wide fabrics. We call for a little extra yardage to allow for minor errors and slight shrinkage.

CUTTING BIAS STRIPS

Strips for curved appliqué pattern pieces, such as meandering vines, and for binding curved edges should be cut on the bias, which runs at a 45° angle to the selvage of a woven fabric and has the most give or stretch.

To cut bias strips, begin with a fabric square or rectangle. Use a large acrylic ruler to square up the left edge of the fabric. Then make a cut at a 45° angle to the left edge (**Bias Strip Diagram**). Handle the diagonal edges carefully to avoid distorting the bias. To cut a strip, measure the desired width parallel to the 45° cut edge; cut. Continue cutting enough strips to total the length needed.

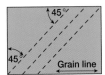

Bias Strip Diagram

MAKE AND USE TEMPLATES
Make Templates

A template is a pattern made from extra-sturdy material so you can trace around it many times without wearing away the edges. Acrylic templates for many common shapes are available at quilt shops. Or, make your own templates by duplicating printed patterns (such as those on the Pattern Sheets) onto template plastic.

To make permanent templates, we recommend using easy-to-cut template plastic. This material lasts indefinitely, and its transparency allows you to trace the pattern directly onto its surface.

To make a template, lay the plastic over a printed pattern. Trace the pattern onto the plastic using a ruler and a permanent marker to ensure straight lines, accurate corners, and permanency.

For hand piecing and appliqué, make templates the exact size finished pieces will be (without seam allowances). For hand piecing, this means tracing the patterns' dashed lines.

For machine piecing, make templates that include seam allowances by tracing patterns' solid and dashed lines.

For easy reference, mark each template with its letter designation, grain line (if noted on the pattern), and block name. Cut out the traced shapes on their outer lines. Verify each template's shape and size by placing it over its printed pattern. Templates must be accurate because errors, however small, will compound many times as you assemble a quilt. To check templates' accuracy, make a test block before cutting the fabric pieces for an entire quilt.

Use Templates

To trace a template on fabric, use a pencil, white dressmaker's pencil, chalk, or a special fabric marker that makes a thin, accurate line. Do not use a ballpoint or ink pen; it may bleed if washed. Test all marking tools on a fabric scrap before using them.

To make pieces for hand piecing or appliqué, place a template facedown on the wrong side of the fabric and trace. Then reposition the template at least ½" away from the previous tracing, trace again, and repeat (**Diagram 1**). The lines you trace on the fabric are sewing lines. Mark cutting lines ¼" away from the sewing lines, or estimate the distance by eye when cutting out the pieces with scissors. For hand piecing, add a ¼" seam allowance; for hand appliqué, add a ³⁄₁₆" seam allowance.

Because templates used to make pieces for machine piecing have seam

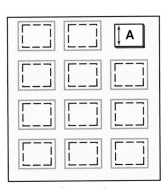

Diagram 1

allowances included, you can use common tracing lines for efficient cutting. Place a template facedown on the wrong side of the fabric and trace. Then reposition the template without a space between it and the previous tracing, trace again, and repeat (**Diagram 2**). Using a rotary cutter and ruler, cut out pieces, cutting precisely on the drawn lines.

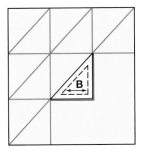

Diagram 2

Templates for Angled Pieces

When two patchwork pieces come together and form an angled opening, a third piece must be set into this angle. This happens frequently when using diamond shapes.

For a design that requires setting in, a pinhole or window template makes it easy to mark the fabric with each shape's exact sewing and cutting lines and the exact point of each corner on the sewing line. By matching the corners of adjacent pieces, you'll be able to sew them together easily and accurately.

To make a pinhole template, lay template plastic over a pattern piece.

continued

Trace both the cutting and sewing lines onto the plastic. Carefully cut out the template on the cutting line. Using a sewing-machine needle or any large needle, make a hole in the template at each corner on the sewing line (matching points). The holes must be large enough for a pencil point or other fabric marker to poke through.

Trace Angled Pieces

To mark fabric using a pinhole template, lay it facedown on the wrong side of the fabric and trace. Using a pencil, mark dots on the fabric through the holes in the template to create matching points, then cut out the fabric piece on the drawn line.

To mark fabric using a window template, lay it facedown on the wrong side of the fabric (**Diagram 3**). With a marking tool, mark the cutting line, sewing line, and each corner on the sewing line (matching points). Cut out the fabric piece on the cutting lines, making sure all pieces have sewing lines and matching points marked.

Diagram 3

PLAN FOR CUTTING

Quilt-Lovers' Favorites® instructions list pieces in the order they should be cut to make the best use of your fabrics.

Always consider the fabric grain before cutting. The arrow on a pattern piece indicates which direction the grain should run. One or more straight sides of a pattern piece should follow the fabric's lengthwise or crosswise grain.

The lengthwise grain, parallel to the selvages (the tightly finished edges), has the least amount of stretch. The crosswise grain, perpendicular to the selvages, has a little more give. The edge of any pattern piece that will be on the outside of a block or quilt should always be cut on the lengthwise grain. Do not use the selvages of a woven fabric in a quilt. When washed, it may shrink more than the rest of the

fabric. Be sure to press the fabric before cutting to remove any wrinkles or folds.

In projects larger than 42" in length or width, we usually specify that the border strips be cut the width (crosswise grain) of the fabric and pieced to use the least amount of fabric. If you'd prefer to cut the border strips on the lengthwise grain and not piece them, you'll need to refigure the yardage.

PIECING
Hand Piecing

In hand piecing, seams are sewn only on the marked sewing lines; the seam allowances remain unstitched. Begin by matching the edges of two pieces with the fabrics' right sides together. Sewing lines should be marked on the wrong side of both pieces. Push a pin through both fabric layers at each corner (**Diagram 4**). Secure the pins perpendicular to the sewing line. Insert more pins between the corners.

Insert a needle through both fabrics at the seam-line corner. Make one or two backstitches atop the first stitch to secure the thread. Weave the needle in and out of the fabric along the seam line, taking four to six tiny stitches at a time before you pull the thread taut (**Diagram 5**). Remove the pins as you sew. Turn the work over occasionally to see that the stitching follows the marked sewing line on the other side.

Diagram 4   Diagram 5

Sew eight to 10 stitches per inch along the seam line. At the end of the seam, remove the last pin and make the ending stitch through the hole left by the corner pin. Backstitch over the last stitch and end the seam with a loop knot (**Diagram 6**).

Diagram 6

To join rows of patchwork by hand, hold the sewn pieces with right sides together and seams matched. Insert pins at the corners of the matching pieces. Add additional pins as necessary, securing each pin perpendicular to the sewing line (**Diagram 7**).

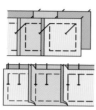

Diagram 7

Stitch the joining seam as before, but do not sew across the seam allowances that join the patches. At each seam allowance, make a backstitch or loop knot, then slide the needle through the seam allowance (**Diagram 8**). Knot or backstitch again to give the intersection strength, then sew the remainder of the seam. Press each seam as it is completed.

Diagram 8

Machine Piecing

Machine piecing depends on sewing an exact ¼" seam allowance. Some machines have a presser foot that is the proper width, or a ¼" foot is available. To check the width of a machine's presser foot, sew a sample seam with the raw fabric edges aligned with the right edge of the presser foot; measure the resultant seam allowance using graph paper with a ¼" grid.

Using two thread colors—one in the needle and one in the bobbin—can help you to better match your thread color to your fabrics. If your quilt has many fabrics, use a neutral color, such as gray or beige, for both the top and bobbin threads throughout the quilt.

Press for Success

In quilting, almost every seam needs to be pressed before the piece is sewn to another, so keep your iron and ironing board near your sewing area. It's important to remember to press with an up and down motion. Moving the iron around on the fabric can distort seams, especially those sewn on the bias.

Project instructions in this book generally tell you in what direction to press each seam. When in doubt, press the seam allowance toward the darker fabric. When joining rows of blocks, alternate the direction the seam allowances are pressed to ensure flat corners.

Setting in Pieces

The key to sewing angled pieces together is aligning marked matching points carefully. Whether you're stitching by machine or hand, start and stop sewing precisely at the matching points (see dots in **Diagram 9**, top) and backstitch to secure the ends of the seams. This prepares the angle for the next piece to be set in.

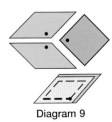

Diagram 9

Join two diamond pieces, sewing between matching points to make an angled unit (**Diagram 9**).

Follow the specific instructions for either machine or hand piecing to complete the set-in seam.

MACHINE PIECING

With right sides together, pin one piece of the angled unit to one edge of the square (**Diagram 10**). Match the seam's matching points by pushing a pin through both fabric layers to check the alignment. Machine-stitch the seam between the matching points. Backstitch to secure the ends of the seam; do not stitch into the ¼" seam allowance. Remove the unit from the sewing machine.

Diagram 10

Bring the adjacent edge of the angled unit up and align it with the next edge of the square (**Diagram 11**). Insert a pin in each corner to align matching points, then pin the remainder of the seam. Machine-stitch between matching points as before. Press the seam allowances of the set-in piece away from it.

Diagram 11

HAND PIECING

Pin one piece of the angled unit to one edge of the square with right sides together (**Diagram 12**). Use pins to align matching points at the corners.

Hand-sew the seam from the open end of the angle into the corner. Remove pins as you sew between matching points. Backstitch at the corner to secure stitches. Do not sew into the ¼" seam allowance and do not cut your thread.

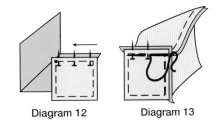

Diagram 12   Diagram 13

Bring the adjacent edge of the square up and align it with the other edge of the angled unit. Insert a pin in each corner to align matching points, then pin the remainder of the seam (**Diagram 13**). Continuing the thread from the previous seam, hand-sew the seam from the corner to the open end of the angle, removing pins as you sew. Press the seam allowances of the set-in piece away from it.

MITERED BORDER CORNERS

A border surrounds the piecework of many quilts. Mitered corners add to a border's framed effect.

To add a border with mitered corners, first pin a border strip to a quilt top edge, matching the center of the strip and the center of the quilt top edge. Allow excess border fabric to extend beyond the edges. Sew together, beginning and ending the seam ¼" from the quilt top corners (**Diagram 14**). Repeat with the remaining border strips. Press the seam allowances toward the border strips.

Overlap the border strips at each corner (**Diagram 15**). Align the edge of a 90° right triangle with the raw edge of a top border strip so the long edge of the triangle intersects the seam in the corner. With a pencil, draw along the edge of the triangle from the border seam out to the raw edge. Place the bottom border strip on top and repeat the marking process.

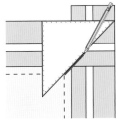

Diagram 14

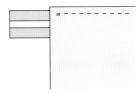

Diagram 15

With the right sides of adjacent border strips together, match the marked seam lines and pin (**Diagram 16**).

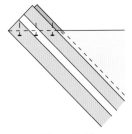

Diagram 16

Beginning with a backstitch at the inside corner, stitch exactly on the marked lines to the outside edges of the border strips. Check the right side of the corner to see that it lies flat. Then trim the excess fabric, leaving a ¼" seam allowance. Press the seam open. Mark and sew the remaining corners in the same manner.

continued

APPLIQUÉ
Start Simple

We encourage beginners to select an appliqué design with straight lines and gentle curves. Learning to make sharp points and tiny stitches takes practice.

In the following instructions, we've used a stemmed flower motif as the appliqué example.

Baste Seam Allowances

Begin by turning under ³⁄₁₆" seam allowances on appliqué pieces; press. Some quilters like to thread-baste folded edges to ensure proper placement. Edges that will be covered by other pieces don't need to be turned under.

For sharp points on tips, first trim seam allowance to within ⅛" of stitching line **(Photo 1)**, tapering sides gradually to ³⁄₁₆". Fold under seam allowance remaining on tips. Then turn seam allowances under on both sides of tips. Side seam allowances will overlap slightly at tips, forming sharp points.

Baste folded edges in place **(Photo 2)**. Turned seam allowances may form little pleats on back side that you also should baste in place. Remove basting stitches after shapes have been appliquéd to foundation.

Make Bias Stems

For graceful curves, cut appliqué stems on the bias. Strips for stems can be prepared in various ways. For one method, fold and press strip in half, then fold raw edges to meet at center; press in half again **(Photo 3)**. Or, fold bias strip in half lengthwise with wrong side inside; press. Stitch ¼" from raw edges to keep them aligned. Fold strip in half again, hiding raw edges behind first folded edge; press.

Position and Stitch

Pin prepared appliqué pieces in place on foundation **(Photo 4)** using the position markings or referring to the appliqué placement diagram. You may wish to mark the position for each piece on the foundation before you begin. Overlap flowers and stems as indicated.

Using thread in colors that match fabrics, sew each stem and blossom onto foundation with small slip stitches **(Photo 5)**. (For photographic purposes, thread color does not match fabric color.)

Catch only a few threads of the stem or flower fold with each stitch. Pull stitches taut, but not so tight that they pucker the fabric. You can use the needle's point to manipulate the appliqué edges as needed. Take an extra slip stitch at the point of a petal to secure it to the foundation.

You can use hand-quilting needles for appliqué stitching, but some quilters prefer a longer milliner's or straw needle. The extra needle length aids in tucking fabric under before taking slip stitches.

If foundation fabric shows through appliqué fabrics, cut away foundation fabric. Trimming foundation fabric also reduces bulk of multiple layers when quilting later. Carefully trim underlying fabric to within ¼" of appliqué stitches **(Photo 6)** and avoid cutting appliqué fabrics.

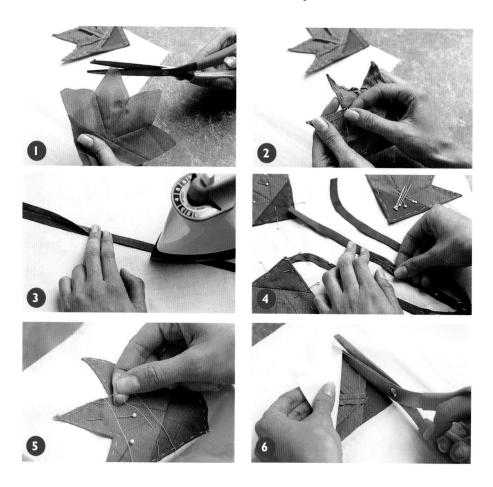

Fusible Appliqué

For quick-finish appliqué, use paper-backed lightweight fusible web. You can iron shapes onto the foundation and add decorative stitching to the edges. This product consists of two layers, a fusible webbing lightly bonded to paper that peels off. The webbing adds a slight stiffness to appliqué pieces.

When purchasing this product, read package directions to make sure you're buying the right type for your project. Some are specifically engineered to bond fabrics with no sewing at all. If you try to stitch fabric after it has bonded with one of these products, you may have difficulty. Some paper-backed fusible products are made only for sewn edges; others work with or without stitching.

If you buy paper-backed fusible web from a bolt, be sure fusing instructions are included because the iron temperature and timing varies by brand.

With any of these products, the general procedure is to trace the patterns wrong side up onto the paper side of the fusible web. Then place fusible-web pieces on wrong side of appliqué fabrics, paper side up, and use an iron to fuse layers together. Cut out fabric shapes, peel off paper, turn fabrics right side up, and fuse them to foundation fabric.

You also can fuse the fusible web and fabric together before tracing. You'll still need to trace templates wrong side up on the paper backing.

If you've used a no-sew fusible web, your appliqué is done. If not, finish edges with hand or machine stitching.

COMPLETE THE QUILT
Layering

Cut and piece backing fabric to measure at least 3" bigger on all sides than the quilt top. Press seams open. With wrong sides together, layer quilt top and backing fabric with the batting in between; baste. Quilt as desired.

Binding

Binding for most quilts is cut on the straight grain of the fabric. If your quilt has curved edges, cut the strips on the bias (see *page 155*). Cutting instructions for projects in this book specify the number of binding strips or a total length needed to finish the quilt. The instructions also specify enough width

for a French-fold, or double-layer, binding because it's easier to apply and adds durability.

Join strips with diagonal seams to make one continuous binding strip (**Diagram 17**). Trim excess fabric, leaving ¼" seam allowances. Press seams open. Fold one end of the binding strip under 1" (**Diagram 18**); press. With wrong side inside, fold strip in half lengthwise and press (**Diagram 19**).

Beginning in the center of one edge, place binding strip against right side of quilt top, aligning binding strip's raw edges with quilt top's raw edge (**Diagram 20**). Beginning 1½" from the folded edge, sew through all layers, stopping ¼" from the corner. Backstitch, then clip threads. Remove quilt from under presser foot.

Fold binding strip upward (**Diagram 21**), creating a diagonal fold, and finger-press.

Holding diagonal fold in place with your finger, bring binding strip down in line with next edge of quilt top, making a horizontal fold that aligns with the quilt edge (**Diagram 22**).

Start sewing again at top of horizontal fold, stitching through all layers. Sew around quilt, turning each corner in the same manner.

When you return to starting point, encase binding strip's raw edge inside the folded end (**Diagram 23**). Finish sewing to starting point (**Diagram 24**). Trim batting and backing fabric even with quilt top edges.

Turn the binding over the edge to the back. Hand-stitch binding to backing fabric, making sure to cover all machine stitching.

To make mitered corners on the back, hand-stitch up to a corner; fold a miter in the binding. Take a stitch or two in the fold to secure it. Then stitch the binding in place up to the next corner. Finish each corner in the same manner.

For more information on Covered Cording and Hanging Sleeves, see Pattern Sheet 2.

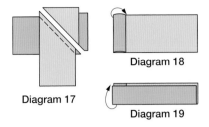

Diagram 17

Diagram 18

Diagram 19

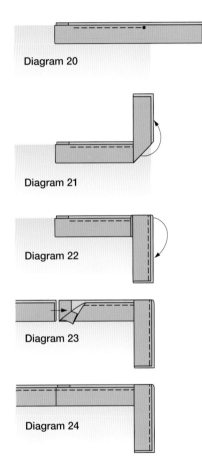

Diagram 20

Diagram 21

Diagram 22

Diagram 23

Diagram 24

CREDITS

Quilt Designers

Round & Round
Judy Clara Blok

On the Dot
Teri Christopherson
of Black Mountain Quilts

Garden Blooms
Becky Goldsmith & Linda Jenkins
of Piece O' Cake Designs

Cabin Tracks
Judy Hasheider

Irish Cabins
Julie Hendricksen
Quilt collector

Mesmerize
Tammy Kelly
of Common Threads

Kid in a Candy Store
Bill Kerr & Weeks Ringle
of FunQuilts

Pierre
Miriam Kujac
Quilt collector

Make Your Point
Mabeth Oxenreider

Prairie Vine
Debbie Roberts

Hunter's Star
Jackie Robinson
of Animas Quilts Publishing

Big-Block Beauty
Pat Sloan
of Pat Sloan & Co.

Tilted Mountains
Nancy Smith & Lynda Milligan
of Possibilities

Majestic Oak Reel
Kay Triplett
Quilt collector

Laura Boehnke, *Quilt Tester*
With a keen color sense and an astute use of fabrics, Laura tests each project in *American Patchwork & Quilting®* magazine by making at least four blocks.

Project Quilters & Finishers
Laura Boehnke: pages 34, 93, 124
Kelly Edwards: pages 18, 28, 83, 144, 145
Lisa Ippolito: pages 64, 91, 104, 151
Mary Korrect: pages 36, 56, 76, 138
Mabeth Oxenreider: pages 47, 84, 118
Mary Pepper: pages 26, 66, 74
Patsy Preiss: pages 115, 152
Jan Ragaller: pages 15, 44, 126
Janelle Swenson: pages 108, 136
Sue Urich: pages 34, 93, 124
April West: pages 108, 136

Materials Suppliers
AvLyn Creations
Benartex
Blank Quilting
Clothworks
Henry Glass & Co.
Hobbs
Indo US
Kona Bay
Marcus Fabrics
Moda Fabrics
Northcott
P&B Textiles
Red Rooster Fabrics
RJR Fabrics
Timeless Treasures
Warm and Natural

Photographers
Adam Albright: pages 58, 84
Craig Anderson: pages 39, 63, 113
Marty Baldwin: pages 6, 22, 50, 69, 72, 87, 103, 122, 123
Kim Cornelison: pages 39, 40
Jason Donnelly: pages 129, 133, 135
Peter Krumhardt: pages 129, 140, 143
Scott Little: pages 55, 148, 150
Andy Lyons: page 104
Blaine Moats: pages 6, 11, 32, 39, 53, 69, 81, 82
Kritsada Panichgul: pages 26, 49, 64, 67, 76, 85, 93, 97, 107, 108, 109, 117, 125, 137, 139, 154

Cameron Sadeghpour: pages 27, 36, 65, 74, 75, 77, 91, 97, 105, 115, 118, 127, 129, 130, 139, 145, 150
Greg Scheidemann: pages 6, 28, 34, 39, 44, 48, 61, 66, 69, 79, 83, 92, 95, 97, 108, 120, 124, 129, 136, 138, 144, 146, 151, 152
Perry Struse: pages 6, 8, 20, 30, 43, 70, 97, 99, 110, 158
Jay Wilde: pages 25, 33, 69, 74, 90, 135